Doing What It Takes:
The Online Entrepreneur's Playbook

Other Titles By Connie Ragen Green

Book. Blog. Broadcast. – The Trifecta of Entrepreneurial Success

Write Publish Prosper: How to Write Prolifically, Publish Globally, and Prosper Eternally

The Transformational Entrepreneur: Creating a Life of Dedication and Service

Living the Internet Lifestyle: Quit Your Job, Become an Entrepreneur, and Live Your Ideal Life

The Inner Game of Internet Marketing

The Weekend Marketer: Say Goodbye to the "9 to 5", Build an Online Business, and Live the Life You Love

What is Your Why?

Time Management Strategies for Entrepreneurs

Huge Profits with Affiliate Marketing: How to Build an Online Empire by Recommending What You Love

Membership Sites Made Simple

Article Marketing: How to Attract New Prospects, Create Products, and Increase Your Income

Targeted Traffic Techniques

Huge Profits With a Tiny List: 50 Ways to Use Relationship Marketing to Increase Your Bottom Line

Doing What It Takes:
The Online Entrepreneur's Playbook

By
Connie Ragen Green

Copyright © 2016 by Hunter's Moon Publishing

 ISBN Paperback: 978-1-937988-29-6
ISBN Kindle: 978-1-937988-30-2

Hunter's Moon Publishing
http://HuntersMoonPublishing.com

Interior Design by Shawn Hansen
Cover Design by Shawn Hansen

Dedication

To the memory of Geoff Hoff - friend, business partner, co-author, confidant. I did not fully appreciate you while you were here, and I certainly miss you now that you are gone. I think about you every single day. Know that your dreams and ideas live on in my heart, and in the hearts of the thousands of people whom you so graciously touched during your short time amongst us.

To Ralph O'Conner - visionary, teacher, friend. You saw my potential from across the aisle at thirty thousand feet and guided me towards a new way of thinking and reacting to the world. I will be forever in your debt for your help, and for the tender mercies you continue to bestow upon my life. May our paths cross again and again, and know that I would go to the ends of the earth for you.

And to the memory of Merrill Hoffman, the man I did not know but whose legacy I have promised to carry on. We share a love of world travel, service to others, and for the city of Santa Barbara. I am committed to humbly following in your footsteps for the remainder of my days.

Foreword

I am so honored to write the Foreword to this book, *Do What It Takes: The Entrepreneur's Playbook*, by Connie Ragen Green. When she asked me if I would write the foreword, I started thinking about when was the first time I met her. I know that it was definitely online, but I went searching in my old Yahoo email account to see if I could figure out when I first joined her list. I see messages from her starting in the fall of 2009, so I have known Connie for almost seven years. I definitely don't remember how I found her, but at the time I was doing a lot of searching for internet marketing related topics. I actually met Connie in person in September 2010 at an Armand Morin event. I was so excited to actually meet her in person. She was just as genuine in person as she was in her emails, teleseminars and webinars.

In the beginning, our relationship was that of a teacher and student. Just like many others, I bought several of her courses and books. Over the years, our relationship has changed and she is now a dear friend, mentor and colleague. She has been instrumental in the changes I have made in my life over the past few years. In February 2013, she asked me to become the 10K Laser Coaching Student. I was shocked and honored. I didn't feel that I had the credentials or experience that the previous 10K students had but she had other ideas. She believed in me much more than I did in myself at the time. Connie has been a constant source of encouragement. I am now coaching beside her in the 10K Laser Coaching program.

Connie was also instrumental in me having the courage to leave the corporate world behind and become a full-time entrepreneur when I was laid off from my job as a Program Manager in October 2015. When I was notified that had I been laid off, I was devastated and was starting to panic. The thought even crossed my mind that I may need to look for another job. I knew that eventually I wanted to leave, but wanted to do so on my own terms. I sent Connie a text message letting her know what happened and she was elated. She quickly called me to let me know what a blessing I had just received. She once again encouraged me and believed wholeheartedly that I would be fine.

Connie has been a full time entrepreneur for the past 10 years. Prior to that she was a classroom teacher, a real estate appraiser and a real estate broker. She started her internet marketing business part time while she was still working, but then she made a very bold move. She quit her teaching job, gave away all of her real estate clients and cashed out her retirement. I don't believe that many people would have been this courageous. As the only one responsible for her survival, she had no choice but to make it work. Connie started as an affiliate marketer and then started creating her own information products. She went on to become an award winning author and mentor. She has been instrumental in shaping the successful careers of many internet and online marketers.

Even though Connie has left the formal classroom environment, she has not left teaching. She has traded in her elementary school students for adult learners. Because of her background as a teacher, she is an expert in explaining business and entrepreneurial concepts that even a "newbie" can understand. She brings the best of both worlds to her students, a former classroom teacher and someone who has actually built a business from scratch. What more could you ask for?

Her teaching includes podcasts, webinars, live courses, online courses and books as well as live events. Her signature live event "Weekend Marketer" is geared specifically to individuals who still have a full-time job and want to get started as an entrepreneur on a part-time basis. Over a weekend, Connie teaches people how to start an online business as well as the mindset required to be successful. She is very supportive but doesn't sugarcoat what is required.

Many people have dreams of becoming an entrepreneur. There is a belief that it is sexy and glamorous to be your own boss and not answer to anyone. People believe they will make a lot of money and have unlimited time to do whatever they want. I am sure you have heard the saying: "I can do whatever I want, with whomever I want, whenever I want and wherever I want." This is eventually possible, but more than likely not possible in the beginning. Connie is quick to tell you that she made many sacrifices in the beginning. She has a saying that she always quotes "Do what others won't for a year so you can live like others can't for the rest of your life". She did just that and now has a life that most would dream of having.

There is a lot of misinformation out there on how to become a successful entrepreneur. If you want to avoid being led down the wrong path, then you should follow Connie Ragen Green. The last thing you want to do is to waste a lot of time and money. You want to be associated with someone who genuinely cares if you are successful or not.

Connie's latest book, *Do What It Takes: The Entrepreneur's Playbook*, teaches you what you need to do in order to become a successful entrepreneur. Connie is someone who has experienced creating a profitable online business from scratch, not just someone writing about it. Connie was not born with a silver spoon in her mouth, but had the tenacity and grit to do what it took to become a successful entrepreneur.

If you desire to be an entrepreneur, then this is definitely a book you need to read. This is not some book based on theory but one based on experience. If you want real life advice on what is needed to have the life you desire as a successful entrepreneur, then this is the book for you.

Adrienne Dupree
Bowie, MD
http://LeaveTheCorporateWorldBehind.com

Preface

Everyone has been made for some particular work,
and the desire for that work has been
placed in every heart.
~ Rumi

Several years ago I was asked to give the Keynote at a large marketing conference in Atlanta. There were several hundred people in the audience who listened intently as I presented my talk on "Are You Willing To Do What It Takes To Be A Successful Entrepreneur?" I wasn't sure how this approach to online marketing was going to go over with this group, but as it began to unfold I realized that I was definitely on to something that was important to new entrepreneurs and seasoned professionals alike.

This was the first time I could remember receiving a standing ovation after speaking. It felt good. I remained onstage for a full minute to breathe in and accept this outpouring of love and acceptance from my peers. It's important to do this so you can recall it later in at a moment's thought.

I went on to give this presentation at another event almost a year later and then on webinars two or three times over the next eighteen months. Each time it was extremely well received and I continued to add to the presentation and allow it to evolve over time.

It wasn't until I was at my own marketing event, Weekend Marketer Live! in Los Angeles, California in April of 2016 that I realized this was a topic that was crucial to the survival and growth of so many people trying to make the transition from employee or even small business owner to successful entrepreneur. This hit me in a split second like a ton of bricks.

Perhaps this sounds quite dramatic as you read this book, or arrogant on my part, so I will explain what happened in greater detail so that you can attempt to see it from my perspective.

My live workshop events are comprised of three days of intensive mastermind, training, and hands-on activities geared to the new and newer entrepreneur. After ten years of experience in this realm I am now much better prepared to give people exactly as much as they need and to persuade them to move out of their comfort zone and into action.

At the end of the second day I joined four of my attendees for dinner and returned to the hotel with the intention of going back to my room to simply relax and rejuvenate in preparation for the following day. As we entered the lobby I could see that three of the people in my group were waiting to speak with me, so I sat down on a comfortable sofa across from them in order to fully listen to them and to hear what they had to say.

I will digress here and tell you that I have become much better at this over the past ten years, and that I now not only listen to what others have to say but truly hear the meaning and emotions behind their words. Instead of thinking ahead to my answer or response while someone else is still speaking, I'm now adept at listening until they have completed their thoughts and then responding appropriately after what they have expressed out loud has fully washed over me and into my psyche. It's a skill that I highly recommend you work on to develop, as it will improve your communications with everyone you encounter during the remainder of your life.

In this case, one of the people waiting to speak with me on this particular evening was frustrated with his repeated failed attempts to log in to the member's area of one of my courses, and the other two were frustrated with not understanding the step by step process of what was necessary in order to set up the sites and the products they so desperately wanted to make available for sale on the internet. It all came to a head at the moment I sat down across from them and I knew I was in for an emotionally charged conversation that evening.

Without going into great details of what transpired over the next several hours that night, or breaking the confidentiality of the people involved I will tell you that during this time and immediately afterwards it then became crystal clear as to what I needed to teach the following day at my event and what I would then come home and begin writing about for this book. What you are reading here is the compilation of my experiences with hundreds of people over a ten year period. The trials, tribulations, struggles, "course corrections", and successes are a direct result of what I discuss here, in hopes that you will be able to connect the dots more easily in your own journey to success as an online entrepreneur.

Table of Contents

Introduction

The best people are like water.
They benefit all things and do not compete.
~ Tao Te Ching

Navigating the waters of online entrepreneurship can be compared driving in New York City to navigating a roundabout in a small town. Although one might seem simpler, or at least less confusing, the next thing you know you're being nudged into the fast lane and crossing the George Washington Bridge into New Jersey.

This ideas and concepts presented and expanded upon in this book were conceived and fleshed out over a period of several years, and are based on the real life experiences of many people besides myself.

In addition, I will be sharing my personal experiences in entrepreneurship here, as well as a step by step blueprint and playbook of what you must strive to accomplish each day as you build and grow your business. We'll discuss both tactics and strategies along the way, as almost equal measures of both are crucial to your success. Five years ago I would have told you there is no blueprint for the road to becoming an online entrepreneur, but my years of working with people around the world have led me to the conclusion that there is a path that will shorten your learning curve and guide you more directly to at least some level of success. It will all be unfolded here in a manner that will astound you at its simplicity and straightforwardness.

Human nature tells us that people will do what they want to do over what they need to do time after time, so along with what you want to hear about the journey to entrepreneurship, financial freedom, and having the time you want to do the things that most please you I will include much of what you actually need in order to achieve these goals. It's mostly about mindset, productivity, and focus, but my ten years as a mentor to people on six continents has taught me that this is the area of greatest resistance and that it's best not to lead with these concepts.

I call the approach "spinach in your smoothie" and I will explain it fully here.

Whenever someone is staying with me, whether it is in Santa Clarita, California at my home in the desert or in Santa Barbara at my home by the beach I offer them a smoothie in the mornings. If they accept, I'll ask them if they like bananas or strawberries, but that's all. I then whip up a delicious frosty beverage and smile while they drink it down eagerly. I will then ask them if they tasted the spinach, and they laugh and shake their head no, they do not taste any spinach.

The truth is that I've never prepared a smoothie without including chopped organic spinach. I'm giving them something they need (or at least something I feel they need) along with something they want. I do this in business as well.

So as you continue reading this book, thinking about what I am sharing, and taking action in various ways, know that you're getting your spinach along with everything else you want as an online entrepreneur.

Section One

Knowing what must be done does away with fear.
~ Rosa Parks

What Is The Concept of "Doing What It Takes"?

Don't tell me it's hard to start an online business. Don't tell me it's hard to choose a niche, set up a WordPress site, create an information product, write sales copy, or do any of a number of the tasks and activities that are a part of this business. Don't tell me any of this is hard because I simply will not believe you.

I will not believe you because we must see everything as relative to something else. I think of something being hard, or difficult or a challenge because it is the difference between life and life, or at least seems so at that time we are living it.

From my life experience, hard is not having a place to live while you are a child and trying to hide it from the kids at school. Difficult is losing your husband to cancer and having two teenaged stepchildren to care for while you are still grieving. Extremely difficult is having cancer multiple times, and then being seriously injured at work, and not knowing what the future of your physical capabilities may or may not be. Challenging is being in a work situation where almost no one has much respect for you and you are publicly humiliated on a regular basis, and yet you cannot quit because you need the paycheck or you will lose your home and not be able to care for your elderly mother.

Setting up a WordPress site and posting to your blog twice a week? A piece of cake in comparison. Creating information products? Writing sales copy? Easy peezy. Hosting a podcast? Authoring books? You can do this blindfolded with one arm tied behind you.

I grew up in poverty, the only child of a single parent and with few family members or positive adult role models living nearby. My mother had barely graduated from high school when the Great Depression worsened and did not have the skills necessary to hold a traditional job. At age eleven I began babysitting and doing odd jobs around the neighborhood to help my mother pay the rent, feed, and clothe the two of us.

By this time I had already survived a broken ankle while playing kickball at school that received no medical attention and had seen a man die after having massive, repeated seizures in the alley behind our apartment building from a heroin overdose.

So please don't tell me anything you must do to start and run a thriving online business is hard, because like I said earlier I just won't believe you.

Always remember that everything is relative and that you have the ultimate choice in what you accomplish each day. Here are some things I have found to be true as you begin or continue your journey to entrepreneurship...

Concepts to Embrace

- Take full responsibility for everything that happens in your life. This was a big one for me, as I was coming from the "victim" mentality for so many years. To finally embrace the belief that I had been and continue to be responsible for everything in my life rattled my core values and beliefs in a life altering way. This included me taking responsibility for having cancer, losing everything in Hurricane Andrew, and even for events that occur so far out of my realm of activities there is no way anyone would even expect me to assume responsibility. Notice the people around you in your day to day life and see how they accept or deny responsibility for the events that occur. This will be eye opening for you.
- Feel the fear and do it anyway. Now this is the title of an excellent book first published in 1987 by Susan Jeffers, and the concept would be expanded upon by Shad

Helmstetter, in his book *What To Say When You Talk To Yourself* a few years later. For years I believed that if you were honestly afraid of something you had two choices. One was to get as far away from it as possible and the other was to grit your teeth, squint your eyes, and try to get it over with as quickly as possible. Now I choose a third choice, which is to face the fear, verbalize what I am feeling internally, move towards and through the experience, and observe the shift that occurs as I get closer to it becoming part of who I am. I've done this with public speaking and working with small groups in a corporate setting and at the Retreats I host in Santa Barbara several times each year. In both cases, feeling the fear as an introvert and getting to the point where I actually look forward to participating in these activities on a regular basis has been a huge shift in my thinking and taking action. It means showing up in my daily life and that feels very good.

- Be willing to die for the truth. This comes from an inspirational talk by actor and producer Will Smith where he discusses how no one could ever surpass him in a treadmill competition because he would be willing to drop dead of a heart attack rather than to jump off while the other person is still on the machine. Now this may sound very dramatic, but the point is a valid one. During my final year of teaching my fifth grade class read a book called *Esperanza Rising* by Pam Muñoz Ryan. Set in California during the 1930s, the title character starts out as a twelve year old girl from a wealthy and well positioned family and goes through a series of transformational situations that challenge her and those around her. During one difficult period, my class had a discussion around the topic of standing up for yourself when you have so much to lose. Now this was before I had become an entrepreneur and began to experience the serious mind shift that would occur. Yet I still found myself on that day stating that I would be willing to stand up for someone in need, even if I would be risking my own safety, well being, and future. Perhaps the seed of what I am sharing with you in this book had already been planted at that time. Whatever the case, it was very impactful to my group of students and most certainly made them take a step back and think about what this truly means.

- Get ready to do the work and make things happen. When the film *The Secret* was released in 2006 I was at the very beginning of my journey as an online entrepreneur. I absolutely adored the idea of being able to think about what I wanted in my life and to know it was on its way to my doorstep. Then the reality set in that I had to actually take massive action and I loved that concept even more. Why? Because I knew that few people would be willing to do the work it would take for them to achieve even the smallest of their goals. That's why I continue to tell my students there is very little true competition for you on the internet, or anywhere for that matter. Do the work, stay focused and productive, and you will be far ahead of almost everyone else.

- Abandon the notion of needing to know all of the steps and pieces up front before you can surge forward. You only need to know the relevant and tangible pieces of any project at the very beginning. This applies to most things in life. For example, when I recently set out on a six thousand mile road trip from southern California across the United States and back again, I only had a loose idea and outline of what I wanted to accomplish, including the cities I intended to visit, the people I wished to see along the way, and the time frame in which I wanted to allow from start to finish. Other than that I was willing to watch this adventure unfold over a two week period. This gave me the opportunity to be creative and flexible and truly enjoy every moment of my trip. Of course I had maps and a GPS system and my previous knowledge and experiences driving between one city and another over the years, but the point I'm making here is that I did not need to know every detail in advance. In fact, that can be a deterrent to success many time because so many things are subject to change between the time you initially decide to do something and when it actually occurs.

- Know that the resistance is coming. Accept and embrace this as a part of the process of changing your life and becoming a successful entrepreneur. This feeling is more than likely going to be a physical one, so you'll have to experience the discomfort a few times before recognizing it for what it is. For me, it's a feeling deep in the pit of my stomach. In the beginning I thought I was either hungry or had a stomach ache. Once I identified it as resistance to change or action related to my business I simply acknowledged it and moved on.

- "Not feeling like it" will never be a reason not to accomplish even the smallest task or goal. When I first heard others saying they did not do what they had intended to do or what was expected of them because they just didn't feel like doing it I was dumbstruck. If you find yourself feeling this way, simply give it a moment and do it anyway. When I need to write a new sales letter for a product or training course or live event I usually don't feel like doing it, but that has never stopped me from completing the task at hand and getting on with it.

- There probably isn't a blueprint for exactly what you wish to achieve as an entrepreneur. Accept and embrace this as a challenge to develop your own blueprint over time as you learn more, implement what you are learning, and experience various levels of success.

Let's get started...

Chapter One

"A lot of guys want to get rich, they want to do it quickly,
but they're not willing to do what's necessary."
~ Edmund Walker to Ned Racine in *Body Heat*, 1981.

The Beginner's Blueprint

Now that I've officially said that there probably isn't a blueprint for exactly what you wish to create and achieve as an entrepreneur, allow me to lay out a blueprint for you as a beginning online entrepreneur.

What gives? I can hear you asking.

The simple answer is that a blueprint is simply that – an outline or framework for your business. It is up to you to flesh it out and make it your own. This will take a period of time. Give yourself weeks, months, even years to create a system that works for you. It will be based upon many factors, including your niche, any previous experience you have, your lifestyle goals, and so much more.

Here is the first phase of your entrepreneurial blueprint, which is intended to get your thinking in the right place in order for you to make that all important mental shift of consciousness:

- Choose a niche that you can work in for a minimum of six months. It will take you at least this long to get the feel for what it means to be an online entrepreneur, to understand the thinking and the needs of your prospects, and to connect with the current thought leaders on how you will be able to add something helpful to the conversation. If and when you decide to switch over to a different niche you will have many "crossover" skills that will enable you to be up and running in no time at all. I did this when I was first online in 2006. I wanted to jump directly into the internet marketing space, but I didn't have the background or the experience to be considered as a serious player to the game. So instead I worked on becoming known as someone who was credible and visible in the eBook writing and marketing space for almost two years before making the transition into what I really wanted to be known for in my business. It was worth the wait, and this period of self-imposed internship served me well when I made the leap into online marketing.

- Begin to learn everything you can about your chosen niche. Do this by reading every day, writing about what you have read, and talking about your position on the topic. Within a few short months you will be an authority and expert on your topic and capable of becoming a thought leader in your own right. Immediately upon starting my business I gave up reading fiction and began reading books that would give me a business education that I could not get by working on an MBA or other advanced degree. Then I niched down even further to read everything I could about writing, copywriting, blogging, article marketing, and eBooks. This education continues to serve me well, as I am almost always able to come up with my own ideas based on the concepts and principles others have had before I came along. This also gives me a level of credibility it would otherwise have taken many years to attain. By voraciously reading, continuously writing, and incessantly talking about your niche you will find yourself completely and totally immersed in the details and able to break new ground with your thoughts and ideas.

- Set up, or have someone set up for you a hosted WordPress site. Hosted means that you own and control your site, as opposed to using one of the free platforms available for this purpose. This website will have a blog, where you will be able to publish your thoughts and ideas on a regular basis. I hope you recognize the potential power in being able to do this. You become a content publisher with the ability to get your name and your business in front of people all around the world.

- Start blogging regularly. By writing every single day you develop and nurture a skill that is of great value. I was not a writer before I came online. It was through blogging that I honed this skill, found my voice, and began to prosper as an entrepreneur. Lest you think this is not a valuable use of your precious time, know that having the ability to reach your prospects and potential clients around the world by simply publishing a few hundred words of text on your topic is pure magic. As you learn more and understand the use of keywords, your blog will become your ticket to helping people connect with you on a moment's notice and massive, targeted traffic will rush to your site.

- Think about a simple product or service you could offer right away to begin earning income. We all feel like we don't have anything to offer others when we first begin, but nothing could be further from the truth. Some examples might include proofreading someone else's blog for typos, explaining how to do something technical, or sharing your expertise from your previous life to someone who will still be involved in that world (this one was eye opening for me as I helped people in real estate with their marketing). Over time you will turn this into a science as you become more attuned and receptive to the needs and desires of your target audience. If you remember nothing else from this section, please let it be the idea that keeping it simple will be the key to your early and continued success.

So this is the bare bones of the blueprint you will continue to expand upon and refine throughout your career as an entrepreneur. Remember that entrepreneurship does not lend itself to a step by step guide as you make your way from Point A to Point B. That would be more of what you'd expect to receive as an employee. The very fact that you must jump in, get your hands dirty, scrape your knees along the way, and forge your own path is one that will set you apart from most of the people you now know or will meet over the course of your lifetime. Instead of following the pack you have chosen to break away and enter new territory for the remainder of your life. Congratulations!

Chapter Two

Focus more on your desire than on your doubt,
and the dream will take care of itself.
You may be surprised at how easily this happens.
Your doubts are not as powerful as your desires,
unless you make them so.
~ Marcia Wieder

Making The Mental Shift

Shifting your thinking sounds like a simple concept, but in my experience it will honestly be the most difficult aspect of becoming a successful entrepreneur.

My thinking was not clearly defined for most of the years I worked as a classroom teacher and in real estate. By this I mean that I was all over the place in what I wanted in my life experience, and was easily swayed by others. It was much more common for me to complain to anyone who would listen about what was wrong in my life rather than to make a concerted effort toward changing my life in even the smallest way. Perhaps I did not believe great change was possible for me or maybe I wasn't willing to do the work, but whatever it was kept me mired in the mud and darkness for far too many years.

In 2005 this feeling began to lift and my beliefs began to change, slowly at first and then gaining momentum with each new day. I was going to be turning fifty that summer, so I know part of this mental shift was set in motion by the feeling that more than half of my life was now over and that I had accomplished so little up until this point. If only I could go back in time and talk to that former version of myself. If I could pinpoint what it was that occurred within my mind it would be so much easier to help others who walk the same path to make the needed changes in their thinking. But I do my best with this and continue to share my story with others. And even though I was starting from a place of unhappiness and negativity, at least it made me pause to think about my future.

Simultaneously, I was introduced to a couple who had made some major changes in their lives. The wife had worked for an internationally known corporation and was caught up in the travel and long hours associated with that. The husband had owned a local manufacturing business that had expanded to more than two hundred employees. Their relationship was strained, they both suffered from serious health issues, and their son and daughter, both in college, had begun to have serious personal issues. All of this took its toll on the family and in the spring of 2005, a month before I met them, they walked away from their previous lives to start anew. By this I mean that the wife quit her job with one month's notice to her employer and the husband sold his company during that same month. I had never known anyone who had done anything as drastic as this and it was refreshing to hear their story and learn more about them.

Their mental shift had been born out of a need to survive. Their health issues were now life threatening and the situation with their young adult children had reached a critical point. They had decided to take massive action to save their lives and their family. We discussed how it took so much to get their attention and for them to start making these huge life changes, and how we should all be open to doing this long before it reaches this point.

I so resonated with what they were saying. And they were putting the changes into action every single day instead of simply talking about it. They cleared out their refrigerator and pantry to eliminate processed foods. They began taking long hikes up into our local foothills and mountains and I joined them every Sunday morning before dawn. The wife began taking online courses to learn more about stocks and bonds and the husband began working towards his real estate license. The kids had taken a leave from their respective colleges and had moved back home to be a part of what was happening within the family unit. It was amazing to watch this transformation and it both motivated and inspired me to do something similar in my own life.

They encouraged me to read and explore new opportunities for my life. This reading ran the gamut from religious and spiritual to economics and finance, and much in between. This is when I learned about online marketing and having a business I could run from my home computer. Even though I had been an early adopter of technology this was all very new to me.

This couple encouraged me to get back to basics by eating healthier foods, exercising more, and reading everything I could get my hands on that would expand my thinking and enrich my mind. I visited the Agape Spiritual Center in Los Angeles with them and was moved by Reverend Michael Beckwith's sermon and message. Within a year it would become next to impossible to get a seat in that chapel for a Sunday service because he was one of the featured teachers in the movie "The Secret". I was in on the ground floor of a movement that was putting people in touch with thoughts and ideas they had not previously explored. Anything was possible in our lives now, even though it had always been that way. I was like a young child, eager to see and hear and taste and touch as much as I could of what the future could bring me. It was exhilarating!

Suddenly it made absolutely no sense for me to stay with two careers, both of which no longer served me. My life became a whirlwind of thoughts and actions leading me to new experiences. I went to a real estate expo with a friend and met my first mentor, Raymond Aaron. I stopped reading fiction authors like Elmore Leonard and Dean Koontz and started reading both spiritual books and books on business. I decided to resign from the school district the following June. I began planning to give away my real estate clients to those who were working in the field full time and could better serve them. I decided to sell my house in the San Fernando Valley area north of Los Angeles and to move to the smaller community of Santa Clarita twenty-five miles away. I was on a roll and couldn't have stopped even if I had wanted to at that point. My mind and thought processes were changing rapidly. I was experiencing something that was bigger than anything I had ever witnessed or experiences. It was...

The. Mental. Shift.

My thinking was clear and I was focused in a way that almost scared me at times over those next several months. My work in the classroom became massively productive as I took on projects and tasks I had previously not been confident enough to explore. It was noticeable within days and others began to comment on what I was doing.

This carried over into my real estate work and my home life as well. I had more energy than I could harness and accomplished so much in so little time. My confidence was soaring and I was on top of the world. I brushed off negativity and doubt like lint from a jacket. I was unstoppable.

Occasionally I would have a moment of sadness and regret that I hadn't done any of this many years before, but that passed quickly as I got back to the business of living each day of my life to the fullest instead of being mired in the past and with what could have been. My future was unfolding before my eyes and I couldn't stop smiling.

Recently I had the opportunity to speak with a friend who is the CEO of an international corporation. You may likely recognize the name, but for privacy's sake I will not share it here. He had asked me about this new book I was in the process of writing and I told him the concept and basic premise of "doing what it takes". He appeared to find this topic intriguing so I went on to ask him what he thought about life and business not being so difficult at all for those who were willing to do what it takes every single day. And I wanted to know what his experiences had been as he traveled the world to interact with people in key positions in other corporations.

His answers and our discussion did not surprise me in the least. He had found that in all of the companies he encountered there were only a handful of people who could be counted on to do what it takes for the duration. He also agreed with me that when you look at the big picture of business the competition is not that great. In his world, where only the best of the best make it to the top, there will continue to be people who make excuses and place blame rather than accepting responsibility and making it happen every single day, year after year, without fail.

Knowing this should make you even more anxious to surge forward and make your dreams a reality. Know that getting up earlier than usual every day to read, write, think, and take action will pay off for a lifetime of accomplishment you can be proud of and enjoy.

Chapter Three

"I'll tell you what you gonna do. You gonna get a job. Some job a convict can get, like scraping off trays in a cafeteria. And you're gonna hold onto that job like gold. Because it is gold. And when that man walks in at the end of the day and he comes to see how you done, you ain't gonna look in his eyes. You gonna look down at the floor. And then he's gonna look around the room to see how you done. And he's gonna say 'Oh, you missed a little spot over there. What about this little bitty spot?' And you're gonna suck all that pain inside you, and you're gonna clean that spot until it's shiny clean. And on Friday, you pick up your paycheck. And if you could do that, you could be president of Chase Manhattan! If you could do that. "

~ Manny to Buck in "Runaway Train"

From Employee to Entrepreneur

Recently I spent time with a group of newer entrepreneurs in a workshop setting. As we sat together that afternoon the conversation turned to the idea of connecting with a non-profit group as a way to network with others. I'm a Rotarian (Rotary is an international service organization) and they were discussing the cost of being a member of this group. One woman said that she had been told that her local Rotary Club cost about seven hundred dollars a month to be a part of, and I reacted strongly to this by saying that the dues were about three hundred dollars a year and that the cost of the meal each week would run somewhere between eight and thirty dollars.

I was shocked in part by the fact that information had been obtained second hand, instead of more directly from the organization itself. But I sat back as the group discussed the pros and cons of being a member of a non-profit group like Rotary. The cost appeared to be the first aspect of this that would make the difference as to whether someone would even visit a Rotary Club meeting in their local city.

I realized very quickly that I was actually witnessing a conversation about the difference between employees and employers, and what it truly means to go from being an employee to an entrepreneur. It's a mind shift that takes some time, and cannot possibly occur until you set your intention and take action on your goals.

When I left the world of classroom teaching and working part-time in real estate behind in 2006, I worked hard at making the transition from employee to entrepreneur. Even though I owned my real estate business, I was far from being entrepreneurial in my day to day activities. The bulk of my income continued to come from teaching, and the employee mentality was a strong one I would have to overcome.

As an employee I looked to my supervisors and administrators for guidance on what actions to take each day. I had some say-so as to what I could do with the children in my classroom, but it had to fit into the structure of what the school's administrators and the school district has decided. Now don't get me wrong here; I had lots of ideas about what would work effectively in the classroom and wanted to share and implement those ideas with others. But the truth was that I was not being paid to have what I considered to be fresh and innovative ideas. No, I was being paid to follow directions and achieve specific results.

Once I left the classroom I began to see things very differently. Soon I was thinking of myself as a creative thinker and everything began to shift. Instead of thinking about how much it would cost for me to join Rotary and be a part of a worldwide organization that could help more people than I could even imagine, I jumped in and got to work. And the interesting thing is that my business took off as a result of the people I met at Rotary and the shift in my thinking that occurred as a result.

An example I will share that might make this more clear is one in which someone decides to relocate to a new city. Does he or she find a place to live first, or find suitable employment before looking for a home? The answer is that the employee gets the job first and then finds a place to live nearby. The entrepreneur first chooses the place they wish to live and then does whatever is necessary to set up an office not far from their new home. Or better yet, they work from home and skip the office altogether. Think about this and discuss it with your friends to see where the conversation takes you and what your own thoughts and beliefs are around entrepreneurship.

Do whatever it takes to achieve your goals. Refuse to continue thinking as an employee who needs constant instructions and supervision and direction as to what to do in each situation. Make a conscious mind shift from that of an employee to that of an entrepreneur and jump in with both feet to discover what is possible in your life and your business.

The late motivational speaker Jim Rohn taught us that we are the average of the five people we spend the most time with. Choose your five wisely.

When I first left my job as a classroom teacher I wondered how I would be able let go of the handful of teachers I had been friendly with over the years. I pictured having to say goodbye to each of them to make room for new people in my life. Looking back I can't believe I ever thought this way. Within the first three months I spoke on the phone and met in person with these people only a few times. Within six months I only heard from two of them and at the one year mark only one of them was making any time for me. It was a natural attrition that occurred once we no longer worked together in close proximity. Soon I was spending time with people who were supportive of what I was doing and knowledgeable in areas where I needed assistance. It all fell into place and unfolded just as it should have at that time and continues to do so to this very day.

Networking with other like-minded individuals is a crucial step in this process. You can't possibly change your life without changing your surroundings, and that includes the people along with the scenery. I value the people in my life more today than I have at any point in the past, and that is very important on many levels.

Chapter Four

Perfection is the enemy of the entrepreneur.
~ Mark Cuban

Responsibility, Confidence, and Perfectionism

There comes a time in each of my books that I write something perceived as being controversial. This is one of those times. So I will begin with the disclaimer that what is to follow within this chapter is simply my opinion, based on my experiences throughout my lifetime. I certainly do not mean to offend anyone, so if you take offense with what I include here please read it through a second time and make an effort to see this from my limited perspective.

Taking Responsibility

I believe that we must take full responsibility for everything that occurs throughout our lifetime, no matter how big or small, and without a thought about who initiated the thought or action or whom else could have been to blame. Failure to do so will only lead to disappointment in ourselves and in our fellow man, and doing so on a daily basis allows for a feeling of pride and accomplishment not often experienced during our daily lives. It's all about having the confidence to accept what happens as a direct result of the thoughts and the actions we entertain every waking moment.

An entrepreneur has the ultimate responsibility for whatever happens in their business. Now this may sound like common sense, but sense isn't quite as common as we'd like to believe. If I don't get the wheels in motion every single day, what happens will more than likely not be congruent with my mission and the vision I have intended for my business. There is no passing the buck, as the buck will always begin and end with me.

This is where I draw a distinction between a small business owner and an entrepreneur. Over my lifetime I have known many people who started and ran small businesses. These run the gamut from professionals such as doctors, attorneys, and CPAs (Certified Public Accountants) to those who run automobile dealerships, hobby stores, clothing outlets, and other service businesses. My own small business, Greenhouse Property, operated for over twenty years as a real estate brokerage and also included the area of residential appraisal.

Those who identify as small business owners become a part of the culture of their business. By this I mean that there is a place to fit in, and to attract new customers and clients who already sought out those services or were at least familiar with them. For example, if you open up an automotive shop to do basic repairs on both foreign and domestic vehicles, people in the area will understand immediately what it is that you offer in the marketplace.

Those who think of themselves as entrepreneurs approach must their businesses in a different manner, in that they were aware of the perceived risk and thought more innovatively from day one. We are in unchartered territory and breaking new ground each and every day. Many of our prospects won't even know we are good fit for them for months or even years and it can take even longer before our businesses can be systematized in any way. We are, in effect, educating the marketplace as to what we have to offer. In addition, unlike the local business we are available to prospects all over the world and may only be limited by the inability to speak languages other than our native tongue.

It is said that a true entrepreneur will work for eighty hours a week to avoid working for forty hours a week in a business, whether it is their own or someone else's. I know I felt that way in the very beginning while launching my online business. Then I woke up one day and had the thought that if I did not take responsibility for making something happen to move my business forward, I was the only one to blame.

There are no employees counting on you, and even the freelancers you outsource to are not solely dependent upon you for the work you give them.

So what does taking responsibility as an entrepreneur truly look like on a daily basis?

As much as I disliked the routines and schedules mandated in my previous life, I have become a creature of habit who now craves routine and structure in my day more than ever before.

Each morning I awake without setting the alarm by six o'clock. There are exceptions to this, but these occur so infrequently there is no need to get into it here. By six thirty I am at my desk in front of my computer and my mini legal pad which contains my "dynamic to-do" list. If I am writing another book, which I do at least once each year then that is my primary focus during the first sixty to ninety minutes of my work day.

If I am not working on a book then I go straight to writing blog posts, putting together short reports, composing emails to my list, and creating content for my ongoing and new information products and membership sites. These are the activities I am engaged in during the first two to three hours each day, and I do this at least five days a week. The only exception is on the days when I am traveling, speaking at events and conferences, or hosting my own live events and retreats. My loose calculations tell me that I am doing what I outlined above approximately two hundred days each year.

Additionally, I host teleseminars that become podcasts, and teach by webinar for my online courses. This takes up about three hours a week on average. I also mentor a small group of people, and that accounts for another three hours each week. I tend to do these things later in the day, so that my prime time hours are reserved for my writing and creating courses and products.

If I don't work on these things no one cares. Family members won't be concerned, the boss won't sit me down for a talk, and the people on my list will not even be aware that anything has changed. No one will call me on the phone or knock on my front door to make sure I am on task to accomplish my goals and meet my deadlines that day. It is my responsibility to make everything happen like clockwork so that my business moves forward in a steady and consistent manner.

Now I am accountable to the people I mentor, but ten years of experience has told me they are the first ones to cut me some slack when it comes to accomplishing the goals I have set for myself and shared with them. They have great respect and admiration for me, which I am deeply grateful for, but they do not hold my feet to the fire in the way that I do for myself.

So who knows and cares whether or not I stay on track, push myself to new limits, and go above and beyond what I have done in the past? Me, myself, and I. And this is perfectly okay with me. Because when I do my very best each and every day, I am able to pat myself on the back and say "Good job, Connie. Keep up the great work. What you do each day matters."

And one last thought on this: Everything we do every single day is preparing us for things that will come later on. When I was teaching in the classroom and counseling my students and their families it was in preparation for the work I now do with mentoring entrepreneurs from around the world. When I was editing and assisting with the writing of students in my classroom and adults in the real estate world it was in preparation for the writing I would do once I came online. Ponder this to decide what you might be preparing for in your own future as you go about your tasks each day. Take responsibility for everything that is and that will unfold throughout your life experience.

Confidence

Taking responsibility leads to greater self confidence over time. And having an abundance of confidence is key to your success, no matter how you have defined what that looks like for you.

As a classroom teacher for twenty years I became an observer of human behavior at various age levels. Two of my years of teaching were at the Kindergarten level, and although this was not my favorite age to teach it did grant me access and insight into what goes on in the mind of a young child who is entering school for the first time.

Keep in mind that the children I taught were from the lowest socioeconomic backgrounds in southern California. Even though the majority of them had been born in the United States, it was rare for them to have been exposed to the English language, let alone speak it fluently, before entering my classroom. That fact alone made them strong human beings and courageous little souls in my book from day one.

And even though I speak Spanish at an intermediate level, it was against federal law for me to communicate with them in their native tongue while on the school premises. Doing so will bring the wrath of the school administration down on you like a ten pound hammer on a threepenny nail. Yes, I know this from my personal experience. But that is a story for another day.

With all of these obstacles and challenges coming at them from all directions, these four and five year old people still entered our classroom each day filled with love and joy and excitement and yes, with confidence.

Their eyes were wide open to take in everything school had to offer and sometimes they were a little too exuberant. It was my job to tame them down a little so that we could get about the business of reading, writing, and arithmetic. The days of socializing during Kindergarten were long over by then, and testing began at the six week mark to see how everyone was progressing.

By the time Christmas, or the "winter holidays" as we had to refer to them had arrived, my little students were more subdued. Their eyes were not quite as wide, their laughter not as infectious, and they were more likely to walk than to run from location to location. Their confidence was beginning to wane and there wasn't much I could do about it, even though I continued to try my best. It was heartbreaking to watch these children's bright and shiny spirits diminish in front of my very eyes.

By the end of the year they were barely recognizable and when I would see them on the playground the following year as first graders they were consigned to the fact that school was definitely not the magical place they had once thought it would be.

That is when I decided to spend as many years as possible teaching fifth and sixth graders. By this time they were completely jaded and disillusioned with life and ready to push away any notions of school being a place of joy. So I decided to approach it first as a place of refuge. My classroom was a safe haven from the storms of life and everyone was on equal footing when it came to respect.

Slowly I chipped away at the buildup of distrust and disappointment they had encountered and showed them that they had the power to determine how they felt on any given day. I would have to say that confidence building was more important that any academic subject I ever taught during those twenty years in the classroom. When they were reluctant to share what they had accomplished with me or with their classmates because they were waiting for it to be perfect, I taught them that nothing will ever be perfect and that we had to fail over and over and over again in order to succeed.

Think about your current level of confidence. Is it as high as it should be? You may be beating yourself up and engaging in negative self talk and beliefs without even knowing it. You may believe that everything you do has to be perfect before others will acknowledge you for doing well, like my students did. That's something else I want to discuss...

Perfection

Finally, let's talk about the illusion of perfection. The reason I say it's an illusion in that it is only in the eye of the beholder and even that is not a permanent state. Perfectionism can be a dangerous state, no matter what kind of work you are doing. Allow me to share an example from my days as a real estate appraiser.

When I would show up at a property to conduct the physical portion of my appraisal I had already spent many hours in preparation. This included learning as much as I could about the history of the property, including the year it was built, the builder, the type of construction and much more. Many times I had already seen pictures of the buildings and even had access to a previous appraisal completed by another appraiser at some point in the past. Once I was there in person my job was to assess the condition of the property on that day and to compare it to other similar properties in close proximity to my "subject" property.

My detailed notes would always include the time I was there, because my valuation would only be good for that moment in time. Why? Because the moment I drove away anything could happen. A fire could break out, a car could lose control and come careening through the living room, or an earthquake could strike. The exact number I came up with to represent the value of that property was actually only "perfect" until I was driving away. Within twenty-four hours the economy could have shifted in terms of the Stock Market, interest rates, and a number of related factors and indices, so this would also be taken into consideration after I left the property.

Over the years I served as an expert witness many times in cases regarding the valuation of property. In one case I was on the witness stand and asked to take a look at an appraisal done by someone else, as well as photographs of the property in question.

In this case the appraisal stated that the property was in good condition, yet the recent photographs showed obvious structural damage. The home was slipping off its foundation and looked like it was slanted at an angle instead of being upright. The judge asked me what I thought and I told him that the appraised value was correct at the moment it had been written and signed, but that at some point in the future the foundation appeared to have given way. I then asked when each had been completed, and it turned out the foundation had shifted to where it was visible to the naked eye only three days after the appraiser had been there. I told the judge that much can happen in seventy-two hours and that I would recommend accepting the value as presented by the appraiser to have been valid on the original day the document was signed. The appraiser was not held liable for damage he did not see that day and the insurance company paid the claim. The perfection of his appraisal had been short lived, as the foundation shifting changed the value by almost half a million dollars.

I myself am a recovering perfectionist. People used to tell me that I was one, but I was too close to my own situation to see and acknowledge it as a fact. It wasn't until I started my online business in 2006 that it came to light for me.

I needed to write, yet I did not want to share my writing unless it was perfect. I had ideas for online business and marketing, but I needed more time to flesh them out before putting them out there for the world to examine. The list went on and on and my business was stagnating. I felt unproductive because I was not producing anything. Fortunately I caught this during the first few months and shifted my thinking.

Once I accepted the fact that nothing I would do in this new business would ever be perfect, and that no one even had that expectation of me,

I was then free to explore the possibilities of pure entrepreneurship. I embraced failure as a means of learning what did not work and to course correct on a regular basis to see what did work. This book is an excellent (notice I did not say *perfect*) example of yet another project that is not perfect but is good enough to share with the world. My goal over these past ten years has never been perfection. I now strive for excellence in everything I do and seek to be ever so slightly more excellent with each project I undertake.

So right now I believe I know what you may be thinking. What in the world does taking responsibility, boosting your confidence, and eliminating perfection from your life have to do with online entrepreneurship. In a word: everything!

Your Path to Greatness

Once you have made the conscious decision to take responsibility for everything that occurs in your life, to work daily on boosting your confidence, and to throw perfection out the window you open up the window of opportunity to achieve greatness in your life. Imagine a world where you are not judged for your failures, where people are thrilled when you make the effort to answer their questions, solve their problems, and alleviate their pain, and where you have the final say as to exactly what will happen in your life each day. That world is one of the entrepreneur, and you are on a journey that will take you to places you could never have imagined. I'm reminded of Dr. Suess and his tale of "Oh, the places you'll go!" I can say this with confidence, as it is exactly what continues to occur for myself and many people I know extremely well. If this thinking is too much of a stretch for you right now, continue reading and return to this chapter another day. Much of this requires faith, and that is something you must come to in your own time.

Section Two

Service to others is the rent you pay
for your room here on earth.
~ Muhammad Ali

Why Is It So Important To Do What It Takes?

I was a person who very seldom did what it takes over the first fifty years of my life. Yes, there were times where I would go over and above what was required or expected of me, but those times came it fits and spurts and not often with any regularity. This isn't something I'm proud to tell you, but it is the God's honest truth.

They refer to what I allowed myself to endure for so many years as "victim's mentality" and I believed this to be my truth. As they say, whether you think it's true or not, either way you are correct.

This all reached a crossroads during 2002 after I had a double-header of illness and injury within a few months of each other. It was a low point in my life and a time that could have gone very badly had circumstances not presented themselves as they did. God was testing me and then placing me into a situation where I had to make some hard decisions as to my life and my future.

The story that follows here is one I have neither written about, never spoken about in any of my speaking engagements, nor shared with more than a handful of people in an intimate setting ever until now. Yet what occurred here shaped my life forever both during and after it took place and that is precisely why I am sharing it with you here within these pages.

Without the events I am describing having presented themselves in my life at the exact time they did, you would not be reading this book today and I would not have been able to change my life so dramatically, affecting myself and many, many people around the world. So please do not feel badly for me as you read the story I'm sharing, as it was a necessary part of my journey at that time in my life. I would gladly relive this experience if need be, knowing now what I did not know back then.

Chapter Five

We are all just ordinary people, capable of taking extraordinary
actions to achieve our goals and dreams.
~ Connie Ragen Green

The Psychomotor Teacher

My twenty years of teaching was with the Los Angeles Unified School
District. During this time it was the second largest school district in
North America, second only to New York, with more than six
hundred fifty thousand students, more than thirty-five thousand
teachers, and more than eleven hundred schools. I taught at four
different schools over these years, and teaching at each one brought
me small amounts of joy and massive amounts of pain.

That was a lifetime ago in terms of my mindset and belief
system. Back then anything that occurred in my life happened "to"
me. I took very little responsibility and felt like people regularly took
advantage of me, were unfair to me, and sometimes even singled me
out and picked on me. Looking back over my lifetime I now know
that none of this was true and that I allowed ninety-nine percent of
what I experienced into my life.

As I stated earlier, the story I am about to share with you here is
one I have never written about and have only repeated to a select
people I know personally.

The year was 2002 and I had gone through cancer once again.
Simultaneously I had an injury at school after falling from a sink
when I was balancing on it precariously to get a bulletin board put
up before I left for the day. This resulted in surgery on my shoulder
for a torn rotator cuff and to my knee for a torn meniscus. Needless
to say, I was feeling pretty down about life in general.

I was out of work for almost six months due to this illness and injury and could not wait to get back into my classroom after the first of the year. Not earning my full income from teaching and unable to do any real estate work during this time had taken its toll on me financially and psychologically.

Just before school let out for the Christmas break the principal called me at home. I was surprised to receive this call, as she and I had seldom seen eye to eye on things during my six years at this school and she was not one for small talk. She was pleasant yet firm over the phone and asked me to stop by school before the break so that we could discuss my return to the school and to my classroom. I welcomed the opportunity to visit the school again after so many months. It had not been allowed while I was out on illness and injury leave.

I arrived at the appointed time two days later. The office staff greeted me in a friendly yet reserved manner and I was quickly ushered into the principal's office and the door closed behind me. Our eyes met across the desk and she leaned in to speak directly to me before I even had a chance to tell her I was glad to be back at school again.

Over the next few minutes she explained that I would return to work on January 2, as scheduled but would not be returning to my classroom. The long-term substitute would remain in that room for the sake of continuity and for "the good of the children". She went on with more details but I didn't hear them because I was more interested in what I would be doing if I were not to be in my assigned classroom through the end of the school year.

It turned out this administrator had given great thought to what would happen when I returned to school. I was to be placed in the position of psychomotor teacher, which was what we called the physical education instructor at Title I schools. In between the psychomotor classes each day I was to find and make arrangements with teachers who would allow me to come into their classrooms and assist with language arts and mathematics. And all of this was to be typed into a lesson plan and delivered to the principal no later than seven thirty each Monday morning.

All of the teachers needed to meet twice each week, once as a grade level and once by Track (we were a four track school open all year around). So instead of the general education teachers like myself and all of the others taking their own classes out for physical education for about thirty minutes every day, the psychomotor teacher took out much larger groups of students for an hour twice each week.

It was never my dream to teach physical education, and besides the required coursework on this topic in order to receive my teaching credential I had not ever thought about doing this. But here I was, sitting in the principal's office, looking at her from across her giant desk, and I had to think quickly as to what would be best for me at this time. Keep in mind that I had been out of work for about six months, earning much less by being on disability than I would have with my teaching pay and real estate commissions and fees, and I certainly did not want to lose my home.

I was forty-seven years old, the sole breadwinner of my household, and the only child contributing to my then eighty-five year old mother's income. So I did what anyone would have done under these same circumstances. I sat up tall, looked her in the eyes, and announced that I welcomed the opportunity to return to school in this capacity. She raised her eyebrows, stood up quickly, and ushered me out of her office.

I remember sitting in my car for a few minutes before driving away. Partially in shock, I wondered how I would be able to do this. Physically I was still recovering from my work injuries and cancer treatments. Psychologically I yearned to be back in the classroom with my students once again. I gazed out on the playground where a group of about eighty students were playing handball and basketball as a part of their psychomotor class. I spotted a man I recognized as one of our regular substitutes supervising these activities. He was the only adult on the yard, as was typical.

I took a deep breath and started my car's engine. Mentally, I knew what I had to do next. I drove to my local sporting goods store, purchased a whistle and a lanyard, and went home to make a game plan that would work for my new assignment.

All of these years later I can see that this was the exact moment where I told myself this would not be easy or enjoyable, but it would be necessary to my survival. I would be willing to do whatever it took to accomplish my goal of keeping my job, doing my best with this new challenge, and learning to cope in this awkward situation through the end of June. Then I would be able to go back into the classroom and all of this would be behind me.

On January 2 of 2003 I reported to school, attired in casual but stylish clothing, including stretchy pants, new athletic shoes, and a hoodie, with my green lanyard around my neck and my whistle dangling from its end. Many people were kind and appeared genuinely happy to see me back at work, while others quickly escaped so as not to have to acknowledge me in any way.

The principal, her assistant, and the reading coach motioned for me to come into the big office, and once again the door slammed shut behind us.

My "office" was to be the old wooden shed out on the playground. I was handed a large key ring and told that the keys to the shed and to a much smaller shed, where playground equipment was stored were both to be found on that ring. They asked for my lesson plans for the week, and I presented four neatly typed pages printed on bright yellow paper. I explained that I had not yet had the opportunity to speak with the teachers about the classes where I would be assisting with math lessons, but that I knew the psychomotor schedule and had included it in my plans.

Without speaking or showing any emotion in their facial expressions, the three of them took turns looking over what I had prepared and then casually handed the papers back to me.

The principal suggested that I go out to the shed now to put my purse away and to see what I needed to do to get ready for the first group of children later that morning.

One additional piece of information I need to mention that is crucial to this story is that southern California is famous for long periods of drought and then shorter periods of heavy rainfall. And, of course, this winter was bringing us the heaviest rains we had experienced for some time. Oh, and one more thing I need to share with you here. Our playground was undergoing renovation, so half of the asphalt was torn up and sectioned off by temporary fencing. Heavy equipment was parked here and there, just waiting for a break from the rain before the workers could get back to their assignments. That was the area where the wooden shed – I mean, my new office – was located and where I was headed to at that moment.

So I pulled the hood on my jacket up over my head, held my purse and book bag close to my chest, took a deep breath, and forged out into the yard. The rainfall was getting heavier and the broken asphalt was more difficult to maneuver than I had expected. Within a few minutes I was soaked to the core, my shoes and the bottoms of my pants were covered in mud, and I wanted to cry. But I didn't. Instead, I told myself that I was still a teacher, able to work directly with children, earning my regular teacher's salary and health benefits, and that I only had to endure this situation for six months. This was me being as positive as I could be under the circumstances.

As I approached the shed I took out the ring with about fifty keys on it. I carefully tried each one in the padlock on the door of the shed, but none of them worked. I started over again, working more slowly and carefully, but again not one of the keys fit into the lock. I did this a third time before giving up, cutting through the cafeteria and out onto the sidewalk, and then making my way around the block to get back into the school through the main office entrance.

When I arrived the principal and the assistant principal were waiting for me. They stood behind the long Formica counter, waiting for me to approach them. Later on I imagined they expected for me to throw down the key ring, raise my voice, and tell them I could not do this job. I would tell them I was quitting and storm out the door. But that's not what happened on that particular cold and rainy day. Instead, I smiled at them and said something like:

"I've tried all of these keys several times but the ones I need don't seem to be on this ring. Could one of you see if there are more keys somewhere so I can try again? I want to be ready for the first psychomotor class so I can get them all into the auditorium quickly and out of the rain."

They turned to look at each other, did not say a word to me, and someone quickly appeared with another large ring of keys for me. They hadn't been expecting this type of response.

This was definitely going to be an adventure over the next six months.

And so the adventure began and the rain continued. A few teachers welcomed me into their classrooms, where I would take a seat in the very back of the room and work with children individually or in small groups. The kids loved the time and attention they were receiving.

The teachers who had never cared for me slowly began to say hello when they saw me in passing. And every Monday morning I placed that week's lesson plan, always printed out in a new, bright color in the principal's inbox outside of her office hanging on her door. And I made it a point to always arrive before she did so that she would see that it was there waiting for her without fail. Someone who worked in the office later told me that she would wave it in the air and show off what she had made me type for her. I realized then she didn't understand that I was simply copying and pasting the previous lesson plan into a new document and only changing a few things each week to bring it current before printing it out. Whereas the first couple of these had taken me a couple of hours, I now had it down to about fifteen minutes to prepare each new one.

During this time I learned as much as I could about teaching physical education to grade school children. Many had special needs and limitations and needed modified activities. Some had medical conditions I was not aware of until they presented while out on the yard. And some of the kids welcomed the opportunity to be leaders in the games and activities I had planned for them. Kids who may not do well academically sometimes shine the brightest when they are playing sports.

Early on I was told there was no budget for additional equipment or supplies, so I did the best with what I had and improvised the rest. I went to Home Depot and purchased heavy rope a hundred feet at a time. At my house I cut this rope into various lengths and seared the ends so it wouldn't unravel. A couple of times I burned my fingers in the process, but nothing was going to stop me from doing the best job I could possibly do for the children. I also went to the dollar store and bought a dozen hula hoops for some games I had found online. Then one of my neighbors gave me about fifty bean bags and my collection of supplies began to grow even larger.

We had lots of balls, including brand new soccer balls, rubber balls in three sizes, and basketballs. These were still flat and in the original boxes they had been shipped in to the school, so I purchased a needle and learned how to inflate them myself.

One day a few weeks into my new assignment some CAL OSHA (California Division of Occupational Safety and Health) personnel showed up and announced that a human being could not be assigned to an office or out building not equipped with utilities or temperature control. The principal then assigned me to a desk in the room where the reading and math coaches worked during the day. I would leave my things there early in the morning and only return later on to quickly grab my lunch and any papers I might need in someone's classroom during the afternoon. Getting in their way was not going to be good for me at this time.

Part of the expectation of having me submit lesson plans was so the principal would know my exact whereabouts at every moment. Sometimes she would come on the loud speaker in the classroom I was helping in and ask for me to come to the office right away. I was always exactly where I had said I would be at any given time so this worked well for my credibility.

One day in February I decided to change things up a bit. My level of confidence was rising and the rain slowly subsiding, so I went up to one of the teachers who did not speak to me while she was on her way to the restroom. She kept walking, her head down and not even acknowledging my presence.

I told her I knew she had a standing appointment every Wednesday to have her hair and nails done and that it was difficult to get there on time because of everything that needed to be done at the end of the school day and after the dismissal bell. I reminded her that I was still a fully credential teacher and could come into her classroom twenty minutes before the bell rang to finish up her daily tasks. I could then dismiss the students and do anything that needed to be done in regards to what the students might need after school. And on my way each Wednesday I could stop by the supply room, because I now had the key to it, and pick up anything she might need, saving her a trip at another time during the week.

Finally she stopped in her tracks, looked me straight in the eye, and said,

"You would do all of these things for me?"

And without hesitation I answered, "Yes."

Finally, after just over a month of getting my bearings in this new position and enduring more physical and emotional pain than I thought possible in a work environment, I had become Red, the inmate from the movie "The Shawshank Redemption". You remember Red, played so masterfully by actor Morgan Freeman. Red was the person who could get you anything you wanted.

So the next phase of "Mrs. Green the psychomotor teacher" was a sweet one. The teacher I just mentioned told her friends, and word finally got back to the principal that her favorite group of teachers were enjoying some perks they had not expected, as a result of cooperating with me. It was a win for everyone, which included the students, the teachers, and especially for me. I did not feel selfish at all, as this was survival of the fittest in this peculiar environment.

The next phase of this part of my life was where I employed the concept of "changing my life one conversation at a time". I had read about this in a book written by Susan Scott and published in 2002 called *Fierce Conversations: Achieving Success at Work and in Life One Conversation at a Time* and wished to change people's perception of me using the concepts she had outlined in her book.

I tested it out with the cafeteria manager, someone who had been in my corner from the day I was first hired at the school. Since then we had become kindred spirits in our quest to make the best of our work situations. We had a conversation one day where I told her about my grandchildren and how I was teaching them about science and technology as a way to further their interests in these areas. Her reaction to what I was saying surprised her, in that she was taking me more seriously than she ever had in the past. I was on to something and committed to having two of these types of conversations, on a variety of topics every single day while I was at the school. This was more effective in changing other people's perception of me than I ever could have dreamed of or imagined.

Soon the principal was counting on me for even more things, such as assisting with testing, sharing my thoughts on the ongoing playground renovation project, and even asking my opinion about upcoming field trips and more. Because I was a credentialed teacher and fully qualified for the recent No Child Left Behind Act (NCLB), signed into law by President George W. Bush in 2002, having me on campus each day was beneficial. Without the restrictions of being tied to a specific classroom, it was possible for me to give my input and even be of assistance in a way that was surreal at times. Even though I was far from becoming one of the principal's favorite teachers that year, she began to exhibit a respect for me that was important to the changes I was about to make in my life.

During the third month of this adventure I began to submit proposals to her as to things I could do to be of further service to the students. One of my early proposals had to do with an afterschool technology club where I would stay after school for one hour one day each week to supervise and assist students in the computer lab.

When she first read this proposal she threw it back in my face and shouted something about not having a budget to pay me for such a thing. I remember this clearly, as if was after school while many teachers were signing out for the day and the office was busy with parents, kids, and delivery people. I reached over and picked the paper up from the floor and pointed to the line where I had typed that I would be willing to do this for no additional compensation. I had never spoken back to her in this tone in the past, and the "new" me was taking over.

You could have heard a pin drop as she read it along with me and then lowered her voice, mumbling something about talking to me about it the following morning. The next day I arrived even earlier, and when the principal arrived we went into her office and discussed this as two professionals would, something I had not previously experienced with her. The result was that the Tuesday Technology Club was born, and within a couple of weeks she announced at our staff meeting that she would be compensating me for one additional hour each week through the end of June to make sure this program could be offered to the students who had a an interest in participating. The times were definitely changing for all of us.

One day I was on the yard with a large group of students when a girl went into a grand mal seizure. I yelled for two fifth graders to help me and told them to run to the office as fast as they could to tell them what was happening. I told them to yell at the top of their lungs "grand mal seizure - call 911" over and over until someone picked up the phone to call. I was not allowed to have a phone with me during that time and none of my students had phones. When I hear about kids and phones at schools these days I understand it from a different perspective. The ambulance did arrive in time to take her to the hospital, but it was very frightening for all of us that day.

Another noteworthy part of this story is how I decided at some point early on to pretend as if this job were paying me one million dollars a year in salary and benefits. I was accustomed to the teachers almost always complaining about our salaries being much too low, and how they would be more than willing to do more of what the administration wanted us to do if we could only have another raise.

So each day I kept telling myself that I was earning a million dollars a year, and when I was asked by anyone to do some additional work my imagination seemed to answer "of course, I'm more than happy to do that for what I am earning at this job". Because honestly, wouldn't we all do just about anything within reason being asked of us at a job that paid that well? Suddenly, being given additional tasks and working more hours seems almost joyous in return for such income. And imagine how appreciated it would make you feel. It's funny how the mind can be tricked and fooled into believing most anything we tell it, and how this enabled me to change my attitude and my behavior. Doing what it took to complete my tasks each day started coming more easily to me and that felt very satisfying. Back then one million dollars a years was worth even more than it would be today, and it made me feel like a million bucks as well to imagine myself being worthy of that amount of income.

If you are currently working as an employee try this out for yourself and see if it makes a difference. Perhaps you have entertained the thought that you would be willing to do more at your job if only you were paid a significantly higher wage. When I increased my salary by more than eight times annually in my mind, it was amazing how much more responsibility I was willing to give myself, and how much time I was willing to spend.

One morning when I arrived at school I had the idea to run around our new track. We had been under construction and renovation for so many months it just inspired me to see the new playground finally coming together. So I put down my purse and other belongings and took off running. A couple of children looked at me quizzically and I motioned for them to join me. Soon we were a group of runners, with the bright morning sun shining down upon us. After several months of being the psychomotor teacher I was feeling more comfortable in this role and ready to take it to the next level. The morning runs continued through the end of the school year.

I could go on and on with this story, but I will save it for another time. When you meet me in person for the first, or the next time be sure to ask me about the day I broke my nose while I was on the yard, or how I was able to visit other psychomotor programs around Los Angeles because ours was out of compliance with federal laws and mandates, or how I handled the insensitive adults, including a school nurse who publicly ridiculed me for providing sunscreen to the kids and explaining the dangers of sun damage to them, and about the time our school was put on "lockdown" because of a police emergency while I was the sole adult on the yard responsible for over a hundred students. I'll also tell you about many other children who had a variety of medical emergencies, again while I was the only adult on the playground supervising so many young children. All of these stories have happy endings, but they could have turned out so much differently with a single misstep.

So even though the yard could be a cruel place, it was also one where some magic happened from time to time. I was there when an autistic boy spoke for the first time after hitting a softball pitched to him, and I wouldn't trade that experience for anything in the world. Tears flow even now as I write about it and recall that moment when he opened up to the outside world. If my teaching experience had only been inside of a classroom during those twenty years, I would have denied myself the privilege of seeing education from a very different perspective.

And the shed? That wobbly, ominous structure that had caused so much controversy at the beginning of my six month tenure turned into a magical place. I cleaned it up and organized the once barren shelves so they were bulging with games, books, crafts, and resources for all kinds of activities. And that's where my students first began to excel in the Presidential Youth Fitness Awards, a program never before brought to our school. Yes, I'm proud of what we achieved during that time, and I know personally that it continued at least two more years after I ended my reign as the psychomotor teacher. All of this is yet another chapter of the positive effects that came out of this situation.

By June the afterschool coach, Jay and I had become good friends and had developed a strong bond, much to the dismay of the administrators. We shared equipment and supplies and made sure the kids got what they needed while they were on the playground.

Many of the students were at school from seven in the morning until six in the evening, and that's a long day even for an adult. Our cooperating and planning together made it more tolerable for everyone.

Even though my situation was improving somewhat it was still far from ideal, lest you think this story ended happily ever after for me at that school. And that's why I planted the seed in my mind that I wanted to resign as a teacher within the next couple of years. Just admitting this to myself and promising I would take action was a huge step.

There is way too much back story with this situation to include here, and it wouldn't serve my purpose of explaining how I came to be someone who was willing to do what it takes to achieve success. I was also going through a very sad personal experience in my family during this time, and the principal continued to treat me badly until that situation came to a close during April of that year. This is still too painful a memory for me to share with the world.

The point I am making is that you can be in the middle of one of the most challenging times of your life and still find the confidence, the clarity, and the focus to be strong. When you reach down deep inside of yourself and do what it takes you will come out the other side as a much better person than you have ever been, and so many people besides yourself will benefit from your transformation.

Chapter Six

I've found that luck is quite predictable.
If you want more luck, take more chances.
Be more active. Show up more often.
~ Brian Tracy

The Future Entrepreneur

No one is born with the mentality of an entrepreneur. These are skills and traits and habits developed and nurtured over time, typically through many years of trial and error, starts and stops, and an awakening of the mind and soul. And when you come to understand these are all learnable skills, traits, and habits it becomes clear that anyone who puts their mind to it by doing what it takes has the keys to the kingdom of entrepreneurship.

I was first introduced to this way of thinking by personal development trainer and motivational speaker Brian Tracy. In 2005 I had the opportunity to spend time with him in a small group setting. That was the year I made the decision to change my life completely and he was instrumental in my decision and process.

He explained that everything we do in business is a learnable trait. I had previously believed that either we had these skills and traits in us or we didn't, so this was quite the revelation. Once I knew that I could become a student of business and success it gave me the confidence and the strength to move forward towards my goals.

There is a quote that was anonymous and I've modified it to be my own over the past five years or so. Here it is and if you've been following me for awhile you will recognize it:

Do for a year what others won't,

live forever the way others can't.

My students and the people who are a part of my Online Marketing Incubator and Platinum Mastermind know when they have begun their year, and will often share it with others in our group. Anyone can do this, but few will continue for a full year. That's one of the reasons why I still say there is relatively little competition in business.

So what will it look like when you make the conscious decision to become a successful entrepreneur? Let's take a look at it and have a discussion of what needs to be done each day.

- Decide what your goals are for the day, the week, the month, and the quarter. Write them down in as much detail as you deem necessary to fully understand what needs to be done. Be quantitative, such as writing "I will write one thousand words each day for my new book, until I reach ten thousand words, and then continue to write at least five hundred words each day. As you are reading this it is a Sunday morning and I'm still in pain from tearing my Achilles tendon two days ago. Even though I slept only a few hours earlier this morning, I'm still here at my desk moving forward with finishing this book on schedule. I may take a nap in the afternoon, as my goal is to write as much as possible during my morning "prime time" hours.

- Have specific projects in the works at all times. These may be small projects, like adding new posts to your blog to build up the content so it will be considered an authority site, or larger ones, like creating a new online course on a specific topic and doing whatever it takes to sell one hundred people into the course. Now this is different than having a million ideas and not knowing where to start. If that describes you at this moment, make a list of the ten ideas or projects you wish to pursue. Then choose the five most important ones in your mind and prioritize them from first to fifth. Now throw away the rest of what you have written down until you have completed at least three of your top five.

This piece of advice may be the best one you ever receive, from me or from anywhere else. If you do not make your most important projects a priority and see them through to fruition you will be running around in circles for the remainder of your life.

- Let others around you know that you have decided to move forward in a serious and determined way and that you appreciate their support and belief in your ability to accomplish your goals in a timely manner. This will be a difficult one if you have the reputation of not finishing what you start or cutting corners when the going gets tough. This was my experience, and it took time for people around me to believe I really had turned over a new leaf and would not fall back into my old ways of mediocrity. We tell people who we are with every action we take and inaction we tolerate. Make sure you are doing what it takes to become both a starter and a finisher of everything you wish to achieve.

- Seek out a Mentor to guide you as you build and grow your online business. Continue to be mentored by others who have more experience, are much more successful than you are at this point in time, and who are doing almost exactly what it is that you wish to do. And when you consider someone as your Mentor, ask them who they are being mentored by presently. If they no longer have a Mentor, keep on looking for the person who will best serve you and your needs. None of us will ever get to the point where we no longer need mentoring in various aspects of our lives.

Once you decide to do what it takes to be a successful entrepreneur you will never have to be concerned with things like not feeling like doing something, or taking responsibility for everything that occurs in your life, or being able to boost your own confidence on a daily basis. Your life will be simpler and much more joyous and you will appreciate your accomplishments in an entirely new way. You will wonder, like I did, why you didn't start living like this years earlier.

And write down or type out my favorite saying so that you will have it close to your work area:

Do for a year what others won't,
live forever the way others can't.

Whenever you have a moment of regression to your former actions, or lack of action, and former belief systems take a moment to reflect on what this saying can mean to you and your life experience.

Entrepreneurs are relied upon for innovation, thinking "outside the box", risk taking, and imagining the world in a different way and then turning all of that into reality. Even if you feel like your thinking and actions are not quite ready for this world, jump in anyways and it will all catch up. Imagine how Thomas Edison, Alexander Graham Bell, and others felt when they tried to explain to the people around them what they were working to achieve. Even Steve Jobs was misunderstood by those closest to him throughout most of his life.

Make a list of accomplishments you were uncertain of at the time you wanted to achieve them. My list includes not believing I was smart enough to graduate from UCLA with honors, thinking that I would never own my own home, feeling like I might be too old to start an online business, not believing I could become a published author, and a whole lot more that I went on to do because I persevered and became singularly focused on each one until I reached my goal.

The Way You Do Anything Is The Way You Do Everything

A couple of years before leaving my previous life behind to come online I attended a series of courses through a globally recognized personal development group. These live events were an excellent way for me to connect with like-minded people and explore what life could me like if I were to be open to new thought patterns and concepts.

An idea was introduced to me there that made so much sense. It was "How you do anything is how you do everything."

I did some extensive research to learn where this saying, or some derivation of it first appeared, but so many people are now using it as a part of their vision statements it was difficult to find in its origin. I traced it back as far as 1999 to the musician Tom Waits. He was referring to his ongoing partnership and collaboration with his wife, the screenwriter Kathleen Brennan.

This concept has turned me into a student of human behavior and an observer of human interactions to see if there is a correlation between the way someone conducts themselves in one situation as opposed how they will behave in another. About three months ago I agreed to meet with a woman who wanted to leave her corporate job and work with me to build an online business that would help to replace her income and give her the time freedom she longed for. We met at a local restaurant one afternoon and both of us showed up promptly at noon. Punctuality is a trait I look for first in people. She then asked if we could walk across the street and go to a different restaurant instead of the one we were standing in front of at that moment.

I agreed, not truly caring where we had lunch. But this was my first red flag that something might be amiss. Indecisiveness is a behavior people exhibit when they aren't ready to commit to doing what it takes. When we had been seated and placed our order she handed me a small brown bag containing some oatmeal raisin cookies she had baked earlier that day. I thanked her for her kindness and slipped the bag into my purse.

It wasn't until later that evening that I took out the cookies to enjoy a home baked treat. There were six cookies in the bag, and each one was different in size and texture. Then I took a bite. They were alright, but nothing special. They tasted like any other oatmeal raisin cookie might taste, and there is nothing inherently wrong with that. But the inconsistency in the size and texture of the cookies was bothersome and got me to thinking.

Was it possible this woman was mired in mediocrity? She knew before we met that I only work with a handful of people each year and that I am seeking people who are willing to do what it takes to achieve maximum success. Here was her opportunity to impress me with her skills as a baker, but it appeared she had made very little effort on this front. How she did anything, in this case baking cookies, was most likely how she did everything when it came to her life and work. If the quality and appearance of these cookies were any indication, she was a long away from being ready to leave the security of a regular paycheck and daily supervision in favor of a life as an entrepreneur.

When she called me the next day to find out who she should make her check out to I told her that it was not a good fit and that I wished her great success. She didn't seem too surprised, as those who do not put their best self forward at every turn are accustomed to being disappointed on a regular basis. If she had thanked me for my time and then gone on to show me, and herself, that she was ready to do what it takes I would have possibly reconsidered. Instead, she continues to complain about her job and how unfair it is that she has to do so much more work than others working for the same corporation.

I am constantly reminded of this idea of "how we do anything is how we do everything." It may seem narrow minded and judgmental to think of people in this way as you are reading this, but if you take the time to observe the behavior and the actions of the people in your life I believe you will come to a similar conclusion. I can assure you that if you do this for even a few days you will begin to understand the wisdom behind it and how it can help you to always be someone who does what it takes.

Chapter Seven

> If I have the belief that I can do it,
> I shall surely acquire the capacity to do
> it even if I may not have it at the beginning.
> ~ Mohandas Karamchand Gandhi

Entrepreneurship Is Worth It!

I cannot imagine doing anything else for the remainder of my life than what I'm doing right now. Yes, things change and our businesses must change as well, but as far as being an online entrepreneur goes, I'm quite happy and satisfied with the life I have created for myself.

Entrepreneurship allows you the freedom to explore areas of your life in new and interesting ways while still earning a handsome living. For example, I recently published a coloring book that is the first in a series of coloring books for adults.

It's called *Coloring for Perfectionists* and it's part of a series called *Color My World Outside the Lines*. And best of all, more than ninety percent of this project is outsourced to people who are much smarter and more talented than myself in creating what I first envisioned months ago. My second one, *Coloring from Above* will be released during the next few weeks and was created in a similar manner.

Where else could you take on this type of project during the course of your regular work day and be both praised and compensated for providing a product that serves others so well? And from inception to completion not even thirty days passed! The joy I continue to experience with this model is greater than I could ever have imagined ten years ago, yet today it is a part of who I am as a human being.

So where do you stand on the idea of online entrepreneurship? Is it clear in your mind? Or are you still thinking more in terms of being a small business owner?

I have shared my thoughts on this earlier in the book, but I'd like to revisit these ideas within the framework of being willing to do what it takes to succeed.

Think of the idea of owning a small business as being *outside of you*, whereas being an entrepreneur is *within you*. Visualize the small business owner going to an office or other location five days a week to achieve the goals of the business. At some point they may hire a manager so they may take off early or arrive later than usual, but basically they must be at their place of business, in person, in order for everything to go smoothly.

Now visualize the entrepreneur waking up with thoughts of how they will proceed to achieve the goals and results that are important to them. Even though they must actually do the work to make it all come together, there is great flexibility as to when and where and how this work will be accomplished. For example, I live in two different cities and also travel quite extensively. During the course of writing this book I was in several locations across the country. In addition to writing the book I was hosting live webinar trainings, conducting my sixth annual Productivity Challenge (more on that later), and connecting with the people I mentor on the phone and through email and social media. All of this allows me to spend the bulk of my day with the activities that bring me the most joy, and in addition to my business these include spending time with family and friends, volunteering for charities and non-profits, and reading a variety of authors as a way to further expand my mind and learn about ideas and concepts I was previously not even aware of in the world. Many days I wake up even earlier than usual, excited to start writing and putting my ideas into action and in a more concrete form.

Can you feel the difference and picture the distinction I'm making here? Entrepreneurship is more about who you are, what you stand for, and how you will get your message out to the world in a way that serves others. It allows you the freedom to think about your vision and to then make it tangible. An entrepreneur's life consists of "time shifting" so that anything and everything is possible within the course of any given twenty-four hour period.

As a classroom teacher for twenty years I had so many thoughts and ideas for projects that would enrich my students' lives and make learning a part of their life forever. But my vision had almost no value because it was not a part of the overall scheme of teaching in the public schools. As an employee of the school district in Los Angeles I had sold out my dream in order to receive a paycheck. It was seldom that I was even asked my opinion, and that became my reality during my tenure in the classroom. It had to be enough to spend that time with the children and guide them through the prescribed, and sometimes arbitrary, lessons each day.

I have no regrets, because if I hadn't lived through that experience I wouldn't be where I am today. But my advice to anyone I meet is to take a close look at what you're getting into as an employee to make sure you can be satisfied with what your daily life will consist of as long as you are a part of it. If you feel deep in your heart and in your bones that it isn't for you, then by all means just say no and move on to what will make your heart sing and your bones dance. You might just be an entrepreneur!

As a small business owner for more than twenty years in the field of real estate, I had the freedom to choose which clients and assignments I would take on, but almost no say in how the work would be completed. We had many rules and regulations that had to be followed to a T, and that made perfect sense for what this business entailed. Creative thinking and actions did not fit in with real estate law and could even cause huge problems along the way.

The only thing I had complete control over was how I marketed my business, and back then my marketing skills were mediocre at best. I did come up with some interesting ideas from time to time, but these were few and far between. As a new real estate agent back in the 1980s I decided to work on some properties available for lease to bring in some income quickly. Our office had the listing on a brand new apartment building with units for lease and I zeroed in on marketing this property. The issue was that it was right next to the freeway, causing me to give it the label of "Onramp View Estates". If you were standing at the front door to any of the twelve apartments you could actually yell at the cars waiting on the onramp to enter the freeway. If their window was rolled down they could possibly hear you and might even yell something back at you before driving forward.

Well this might be funny, but for most people this would not be an ideal living arrangement. So I thought outside the box and advertised these units for their true benefits; they were close to the freeway, brand new, and priced competitively. On a Saturday morning about eight people showed up at my office in response to my ad, and we proceeded to caravan the few blocks over to the building. One by one they dropped out of the running. Two men were left standing there and it turned out they were the general contractors for a new shopping center that would be build just a few blocks away over the course of the next year. They needed apartments for themselves and for some of their workers that were clean, conveniently located to the job site, and affordably priced. They leased all of the until in this building for one year, and I received a hefty commission check within the next couple of weeks. Even the manager of the real estate office I was working with at that time was amazed at my results. Another agent, upon hearing about what I had done said that it reminded him of himself at a younger age.

This was my first brush with anything that resembled entrepreneurship and I longed for more. But it took me many years to understand that only I could make this happen. Now I understand that we can have anything we want as a part of our life experience if we are clear about the goals and outcomes we wish to achieve and are willing to do whatever it takes to get from where we are currently to where we would prefer to be in our lives.

Courageous Entrepreneurs

Some of the smartest and most courageous people I know are entrepreneurs. In fact, this group of people is outstanding in so many ways I am humbled to be amongst them. I'd like to introduce you to a few of them here.

I first met Adrienne Dupree in person at a live marketing event in

Atlanta in 2010. She had already been on my list for at least a year at that time, but when we met in person I could instantly see that she was someone special. She carried herself with an air of poise and confidence that typically comes from being raised in a home with values and beliefs that instill great respect and emphasize the need to think of others first.

Adrienne is also what we refer to as "wicked smart" and that is an added bonus when you want to start any type of business. Perhaps I place great value on this characteristic because I am only slightly above average in intelligence and can't even aspire to this level during my lifetime. Instead, I choose to surround myself with people of this caliber.

Over these past few years I have watched her as she dealt with her corporate jobs in the most professional way. It turned out that she was allocated (a phrase I had not been familiar with) at one hundred fifty percent at times, meaning that Adrienne was expected to work sixty hours in order to get the work done, while only being paid for forty hours. Rather than to ever complain, instead she did whatever it took to meet the deadlines and achieve the goals the company assigned to her and her team. I have the highest respect for her because of her commitment to excellence during these years, while simultaneously working well into the wee hours of the morning many times in order to build her online business.

At the end of 2015 Adrienne was able to leave the corporate world behind and come online full time. Her business continues to grow as a result of her daily efforts to do what it takes to achieve her goals.

Dennis Becker and I were first introduced when one of my clients sent out an email about his *Five Bucks a Day* eBook. For the remainder of that day I devoured its contents, and I knew this was someone I wanted to learn from and get to know much better.

I now consider Dennis as one of my friends and mentors who is always available to listen to my ideas and marketing strategies. He makes me work harder and enable me to see my business from a new perspective on a regular basis, and this is based on his own experiences.

He used to run a brick and mortar business in a small town in

Bergen County, New Jersey, one that specialized primarily in sports memorabilia and collectibles. He and his wife ran the store for years, but had finally had enough after a series of mishaps that I won't go into here. After that Dennis shifted his focus and energy to selling on eBay and had some moderate success there. Around the turn of the century he came online, and it wasn't too long after that he wrote his now famous *Five Bucks a Day* eBook.

Soon after he started his Earn 1K a Day Forum and that attracted some of the biggest names working online, but long before they became big names.

When I found out about Dennis in 2010 I knew this was someone I wanted to learn from and get to know better. The rest is history, and I have spoken at his live marketing events many times as well as being one of his top affiliates consistently over the past five years or so.

Marlon Sanders is a legend on the internet, having come aboard during the mid 1990s with advertising on the AOL platform and creating digital products that were revolutionary and innovative. He is a true pioneer who paved the way for people like me to enjoy the lifestyle afforded by this business model.

He and I speak by phone on a regular basis, and I feel like I've had a crash course in marketing each time we speak. I gave him a personalized ring tone on my phone, because I know when I answer that I better be sitting in front of my computer taking notes for the next couple of hours.

Marlon has an uncanny sense about what is happening in the world of online marketing, and perhaps this can be attributed to his vast experience and longevity. He's seen and done it all, so if you have questions about something you perceive as being new and different he can set you straight pretty quickly and save you lots of time and energy.

While waiting in line at the post office in Santa Clarita, one of the two cities I call home, I found myself talking to a lady who was simply captivating. When we worked our way to the front of the line and went to separate windows I found myself longing to spend more time getting to know her. I had told her a little bit about what I was doing online in my business and she had said that she was involved with something similar.

I waited for what seemed like an eternity, and almost left two different times. Finally she was finished with her transaction and did not seem in the least surprised to see that I had waited for her. I thrust my card into her hand and asked her to please contact me so that we could meet to talk some more. She did just that and we have now become friends. This woman is Barbara Winter, entrepreneur and author of *Making a Living Without a Job - Winning Ways for Creating Work That You Love*. It turned out that many people on my list were already on her list and it was the kind of coincidence that happens to me on a regular basis these days.

Barbara's branding is Joyfully Jobless and she has been at this for more years than just about anyone I know. If I had met her many years ago my life may have taken a very different path, but we must appreciate the journey we are on and learn everything we can from it.

She talks about being persistent in your efforts, embracing the repetition, setting goals, and reframing your current job, if you still have one.

I did this during my last year as a teacher and share this story with you during Chapter Five of this book. I pretended that it was paying me one million dollars a year in salary, and that I needed to do everything possible to be worthy of that kind of paycheck. I began seeing myself more as a service provider than as an employee and it was noticeable from day one. Taking ownership of my duties and responsibilities made me see everything I was doing and expected to do in a very different light, and this was, well, enlightening.

So there you have four of the entrepreneurs I most admire. They are as diverse as four people can be, and I attribute that to the fact that entrepreneurs are unique individuals who are all cut from a different cloth. We see the world differently from those to choose to walk a different path. Sometimes we can be misunderstood, but once you take the time and make the effort to tune in to our frequency the doors fling open to a world of magic and possibilities. Come soar with us, if you dare!

Section Three

Step out of the history that is holding you back.
Step into the new story you are willing to create.
~ Oprah Winfrey

What If You Do What It Takes?

I will continue to say and firmly believe there is very little competition for entrepreneurs. And this isn't restricted to the world of online entrepreneurship. In fact, there is very little competition in any area of business. It's a level playing field, where you can and will excel simply by showing up, taking an interest in what you are doing, learning as much as you can, and implementing what you learn every single day. This is what the "doing what it takes" principle looks like in the reality of today's business world.

You have most likely known people all of your life who have this mentality and exhibit it in their everyday life. They are the first ones to volunteer for a project, help someone in need, or take responsibility for something others wish to push aside. They are energetic, enthusiastic, go-getters whom we all wish to emulate. It's almost as though they know a secret to life that's just out of grasp for the rest of us. And this boundless energy and willingness to serve others can be contagious for those wishing to make some major changes in their life very quickly.

It turns out we can all have this same attitude and the ensuing results once we commit to living in this way. Daily life becomes more joyous, as opposed to it being a struggle and a challenge at every turn. More opportunities present themselves and everything we wish to achieve becomes just a little bit easier and noticeably smoother. You will even find yourself smiling for no apparent reason, something that can seem peculiar to a bystander not in the know. I think of myself and those around me who are achieving great success as being "ordinary people striving for extraordinary results". You can be part of this group if you strive for excellence, not perfection, every single day.

Is it honestly as simple as this? Yes. Will you be more likely to experience these results after reading this book? Yes. Will everyone take advantage of this? No. Remember there is very little competition, because most people will not be willing to do what it takes consistently. If you do, you will reap the rewards and most likely never return to your previous self. Here's to hoping you do exactly this...

Chapter Eight

> The only thing I see that is distinctly different
> about me is I'm not afraid to die on a treadmill.
> I will not be out-worked, period.
> You might have more talent than me, you might be
> smarter than me, you might be sexier than me,
> you might be all of those things.
> But if we get on the treadmill together, there's two things: You're
> getting off first, or I'm going to die.
> It's really that simple, right?
> ~ Will Smith

Massive Productivity By Doing What It Takes

Doing what it takes will exponentially increase your results. What does this actually mean? Let's take a closer look.

Doing what it takes in your life and in your business means taking the initiative to make sure things happen. It means getting out of bed when you first open your eyes each morning, no matter how early it is. I haven't set an alarm to wake me up in many years because my mind and my body are always on high alert to jump out of bed and start working as soon as I am rested from my night's sleep.

These actions, whether large or small, on a daily basis will lead to massive productivity. As I type this it is just before five in the morning. I am fully rested and refreshed after seven hours of sleep and ready to take on the day. My goal right now is to write a minimum of one thousand words for this book, and to then move on to other tasks and activities in my personal life and for my business. Doing what it takes each day means I *get* to do these things, not that I *have* to do them or anything else during the course of my day.

The rewards are great and many from living your life in this way. You virtually destroy your competition because no one can do as much as you can do or last as long as you can. In college I joined the track team and was quite successful, considering I have never even thought of myself as an athlete. My times were just average for running short distances of fifty or a hundred yards. We joked that I wasn't quite dashing, but more like sauntering.

But when it came to half and full marathons, that was a different story. I would come to the event fully rested and both mentally and physically prepared. I also had the correct clothing and footwear for what I was engaging in with my track events. And when I left the starting line I had a single focus as to what I wanted to achieve. I kept my mind's eye fixated on the prize of finishing the race in the shortest period of time humanly possible. Others would fall out early, or allow themselves to slow down at various places, but I just kept on going. That's where I first developed the reputation of being both a starter and a finisher.

Somehow I lost my way on this path during the middle of my life, but when I left my previous life behind to come online full time in 2006 it all came rushing back to me. I was willing to do whatever it would take to achieve exponential success through massive productivity.

The Mentored Life

Doing what it takes means that you will try whatever your mentor suggests, even if you don't think it's a good idea, don't want to do it, or don't think you are capable of achieving what they are asking you to do. If you trust them enough to have taken them on as a mentor, then you know they will only guide you to greatness and never ask you to do something they themselves would not be willing to do. They can see you as you cannot see yourself. My mentors have led me to achieving goals I didn't even know I wanted to set for myself. That's how I began writing every single day, creating information products at the rate of one per month, speaking at live events on several different topics, authoring my first book, and hosting my first live event. Later on I expanded my horizons and wrote more books, taught online courses, spoke on different continents, and began hosting larger marketing events, and smaller Retreats in Santa Barbara. Mentors can give you the confidence and the courage to do what you thought could not be done. Believing in yourself is the greatest gift, but someone else must believe in you first if you are to see and believe in that part of yourself forever after.

Doing what it takes means that you have super powers. I can accomplish more in one day than most people can in one month. I just keep on moving, solving problems and achieving excellent results in the process.

Many years ago I was told by someone in my real estate office that if you want something done, ask the busiest person in the office. I questioned this line of thinking at the time, as it just didn't make sense to my way of thinking. Why wouldn't I ask the person who had lots of free time to help me with my project? The answer soon became clear. The person with extra time wasn't good at taking on new tasks and getting them done. They would plan and think and analyze to the point of exhaustion. The busiest person simply added the task to their list and proceeded in getting it done. They were also excellent at delegation, a skill I had yet to master. These were an effective strategies that I embraced and benefitted from.

It's All Relative

Massive productivity is relative. Once you have stepped up your game and are achieving more each day you can never go back to only doing as much as you used to do each day. Your mind will cooperate by finding shortcuts, helping you to delegate what is better done by someone else, and increasing your level of energy. You will have heightened awareness and increased creativity as you move through your day. This will lead you to being perceived as charismatic, clever, and smarter than the average person. Doing what it takes transforms you into the most interesting person in the room.

I continue to find that very few people I meet are able to keep up with me. I don't mean physically, because my pace is slow and steady and determined. But mentally, I am able to jump from task to task to task seamlessly, especially during my morning prime time hours. You will be able to do the same thing once you have practiced this strategy for a period of time.

Also, just in the process of being productive each day you will rack up more hours of experience than others. This is part of something called the "10,000 Hour Rule" which I have discussed in great detail in my previous books. It's based on research from psychologist Anders Ericsson and applies to what I am sharing with you here.

You must go back to the time when you were a daydreamer. For most of us that is around the age of five or six, before parents and teachers and other well meaning adults forced us to snap out of it. I am thankful I never did this to a child in my life or in one of my classrooms.

I remember a conversation I had with the Reading Specialist at the last school where I taught. Her son was about twelve and she had come home one day to find him sitting on the sofa and gazing into space. She snapped her fingers in front of his face, startling him to the point where he almost fell off the sofa. She then told him that it was never okay to be doing "nothing" and that he must always be engaged in an activity. I shuddered while listening to her tell this story, silently saying a prayer that her son would find other adults who did not feel this way. He had been daydreaming and was admonished for this behavior. Imagine if the greatest people of all time had not been allowed this simple mental freedom on a regular basis. Perhaps our world would not be as filled with music, literature, art, writing, technology, and the other joyous gifts and enhancements we value so greatly if the people who gave them to us had been forced into rigid thinking at all times.

Doing what it takes means standing up for yourself and for others even when it is uncomfortable and unpopular, understanding the difference between right and wrong and making amends when you realize you were wrong, and thinking more about what *could be* than about what actually *is*. It means acknowledging what is realistic and then moving on to greatness. It means living each day as though it were to be your last and having no regrets. I am reminded of the Tim McGraw song where he sings "I hope you have the chance to live like you were dyin'".

Once you can accept and embrace what it means to achieve massive productivity by doing what it takes, all fear and doubt falls away as you get on with the business of living.

Rocks, Pebbles, Sand, Water

You may already familiar with this analogy. I have written about it in two of my previous books but it is definitely worth revisiting here for the lessons and examples it provides.

Once upon a time in a land not so far away there was a philosophy professor who was giving a lecture on the topics of time management, choices, and priorities. He wanted to make the point that we all have free agency in most everything we do in our lives. He had placed a large glass jar on the table in front of him. He started off by filling up the jar with big rocks and when they reached the rim of the jar he held it up to the students and asked them if the jar was full. They all agreed, there was no more room to put the rocks in because it was already full.

He then picked up a tub of small pebbles and poured these in jar so that they filled the space around the big rocks. "Is the jar full now?" he asked. The group of students all looked at each other and then agreed that the jar was now completely full.

The professor then picked up another container, this time one that had sand in it. He poured the sand in between the pebbles and the rocks and once again he held up the jar to his class and asked if it was full. Once again the students agreed that the jar was full.

"Are you sure it's full?" he asked.

He finally picked up a bottle of water and allowed it to flow into the jar until it filled up all the remaining space. The students laughed. The jar represents your life. The rocks are the important things that have real value – your family, your health, your faith, and the other special people in your life – things that if everything else was lost and only they remained, your life would still be full.

The pebbles are the other things that matter – like your business, your home, and so forth. The sand is everything else in your life, all of the smaller, more insignificant stuff.

If you fill the jar up first with the sand, you won't have space for the pebbles or the rocks. The same goes for your life. If you spend all your time and energy on the small stuff, you will never have room for the things that are important to you. Pay attention to the things that are critical to your happiness. Play with your children. Spend time with your family. Go out dancing. Go for a good meal. There will always be time to work, clean the house, give a dinner party, and fix the disposal. Take care of the rocks first – the things that really matter to you. Set your priorities. The rest is just sand.

I prioritize by marking my calendar each month with my rocks first and then my pebbles. That leaves plenty of time for my sand and my water, without taking time away from the things that matter most to me. Guarding and protecting my time has put my life into perspective. It also has taught me that I am not seeking "balance" at all, but instead a schedule that allows me to make the choices as to how, where, and with whom I will spend my time each and every day.

Chapter Nine

The first person you are accountable to is yourself.
It's imperative that you know what your key
values are, because they set the standards
for how you will do business.
~ Marilyn Strong

What Is Actually Possible?

My dream back in 2006 was to be able to replace the current income I received by working for the school district as a classroom teacher and in my real estate business as a broker and residential appraiser with income I could earn on the internet from the comfort of my own home. It was a lofty goal for me at that time, but one I believed in strongly after observing what so many others at least appeared to be doing.

At that time I had full access to public records from across the United States, so I searched the names of the people working online who were making large income claims to see if they could be justified. It had been my experience over the previous twenty years that when someone began earning more income they were more likely to purchase more real estate, including a nicer home for themselves and their families, income producing properties, and investment properties.

The public records did not let me down, and after searching through about a dozen names I was convinced this was a legitimate business that paid off handsomely. Person after person came up as the owner of multiple real estate holdings. This quickly led to my decision that I would be willing to spend time every single day in doing whatever it took to make my dream of online entrepreneurship a reality. This was exactly the information I needed in order to move forward with excitement, enthusiasm, and a new work ethic.

Without sharing my current income with you here suffice it to say that there is no job I could hold or business I could start that would afford me the lifestyle I now enjoy.

As an entrepreneur we set our own schedules and engage in the tasks and activities that are income producing on a daily basis. This is what I think about when I first get started in the morning, throughout the day, and before going to sleep at night. As long as what I am doing will produce income at some point today or in the future, then it is a worthwhile activity to pursue. Sometimes I have to stop and think about this to see if I am inspired or motivated for other reasons. This is acceptable, as long as I acknowledge the facts and keep moving forward.

For example, each year I host what I refer to as a "Productivity Challenge" on my blog. I have included my most recent one as an example in the Appendix at the end of this book. I've done this every year since 2011, and in the beginning I questioned whether this could be turned into an income producing activity or not. I was willing to take my time in building this up so that it would be a viable use of time and resources, as well as being beneficial to those who would participate along with me.

The results now are quite amazing. I have perfected this strategy to the point where I am able to host a challenge in only ten minutes a day over the course of the thirty days. I then repurpose the content from the challenge into a new product, a free giveaway, and even part of my book. The ROI (return on investment) continues to grow and my own students are then inspired and motivated to host their own challenges.

The point I am making here is that initially it may take some time for your ideas and hard work to pay off, but if you believe they come from solid stock be willing to nurture them into a hearty soup worthy of sharing with the world.

The possibilities are endless when you are an entrepreneur. Remember that I was not a writer before coming online and continue to type with my two index fingers. This has not stopped me from authoring more than a dozen bestselling books, writing thousands of articles and blog posts, and being thought of as a writer who matters in the world of marketing and entrepreneurship. My two fingers have resulted in more than a million words of writing so far! Always be willing to do what it takes to achieve what you most want in your life. You will be unstoppable and no one will be able to catch you because there is no competition at the top.

Believe in yourself and in the power you have to change and shape your life one day at a time. Think about the story I shared in Chapter Five about the six month period where I was the physical education teacher and how that experience gave me the confidence and the courage to leave the teaching profession for good after twenty years. You can do, have, and be anything and anyone you want to be, and it all begins when you plant the seed in your mind and then take the necessary and inspired action to put it into motion. if you aren't clear about where you want to go exactly, start from where you are and take the next logical step towards a life that will better serve you and your dreams.

Chapter Ten

I miss 100% of the shots I don't take.
~ Wayne Gretsky

Reaching Your Full Potential

The concept of someone having the wherewithal to reach their full potential is an often misunderstood one. I was first introduced to it as a new classroom teacher back in the 1980s in regards to the students' ability to be the best they could be academically.

There was not a holistic approach to teaching at that time, and the fact that someone might excel in sports or be a creative thinker or show leadership qualities was never considered. Everything was about the academic subjects of language arts, social studies, science, and mathematics. If you could attain perfect scores on the objective exams and then score in the top percentiles for the state testing it was said that you had reached your full potential. Obviously, this was a rare occurrence and a goal few even aspired to for that very reason. The unattainable is often discarded in favor of a more subjective view and approach, and this was the ongoing battle between the classroom teachers and the administration while I was a part of this profession.

Of course, I was the controversial one when I wrote something about one child's potential in terms of their creativity in writing and their artistic talent on their final report card. It was true, and that student went on to achieve great things in these areas over the next several years. In fact, he even worked briefly at Lucas Film in northern California, the studio founded by filmmaker George Lucas of Star Wars fame.

Reaching one's full potential as an entrepreneur is somewhat more abstract. Everyone chooses their own path and travels at their own pace. There are no measuring devices in place, other than the metrics of traffic, sales, and income. Concepts without borders like "imagining", "visualizing", and "creating" are tossed into the mix, further confusing the logical mind.

So where will you fit in along this continuum? My recommendation is to not even try. If you've come from a background of being an employee or even owning and operating a small business then you'll want to walk a different road, forge your own path, and develop your own set of rules. The metrics I mentioned above will keep you grounded in the reality, but don't get bogged down with numbers and systems.

And most definitely you do not want to compare yourself with others, as no one wins in that scenario. For the first time, perhaps ever in your life you will need to nurture and encourage your intuition to lead you to what others may say is "your full potential". And in all things business and personal, do whatever it takes to accomplish your goals, immediately create and set even bigger goals, and let your conscience and inner voice be your guide.

While I was in the classroom we were evaluated each year using something called the "Stull Evaluation". This continues to be used and is based on the Stull Act, first signed into law by then Governor Ronald Reagan back in 1971. It is further explained in the California Education Code, Section 44660-44665. It was originally based on the theory of being able to freeze a moment in time and to then be able to make a determination as to how things were done throughout the school year. This did not work so well, in my personal opinion. Nothing I did in the classroom day in and day out could be encapsulated into a single and specific "moment in time".

If you are anything like me and the people I continue to mentor, getting the corporate world, or wherever you were working before coming online out of your head will take some time. I believe it was a full year before I could develop a schedule for myself and think about reaching my full potential on my own terms. After years of evaluations of my work by people who did not understand what it meant to spend thirty hours each week with children of a certain age, I was ready to move away from that belief system and to start making my own rules.

The human brain is a powerful organ, capable of more than any computer will ever be able to achieve. Reach deep into the recesses of your mind and know that you can do, be, and have anything that you want. Yes, this will require you to do what it takes to make it all come together, but that is a small price to pay for the joy that will come from seeing your work come to fruition.

You are creating your "body of work" as a blueprint and playbook for this lifetime and as a legacy for generations to come. When that notion was first presented to me it seemed surreal, but once I got my mind around the idea it make perfect sense. if you remember the film "Mr. Holland's Opus" you know that Mr. Holland was the high school music teacher who thought he had given up his dream of becoming a classical composer in favor of having a family and accepting the responsibilities that come along with that lifestyle. In truth, he had been creating his masterpiece - his opus - all along and was finally acknowledged for his lifetime of great work. Acknowledge yourself silently or out loud each day to celebrate what you are accomplishing over time.

As he conducted his music at the end of the film you can't help but feel like Mr. Holland lost many years in thinking and believing that what he was doing didn't matter instead of knowing and understanding that everything we do is leading us to the next stages of our life and our business. Little did I know when I wrote my first two hundred fifty word article back in 2006 that by 2010 I would begin publishing books that would help so many people to understand the ideas of online entrepreneurship. What is your opus?

Potentially (please pardon my pun) you could achieve more over the years of your life still remaining than you could have in several lifetimes without making this mental shift and taking action on it. Now that, dear reader, is truly reaching your full potential.

Chapter Eleven

It is time for us all to stand and cheer for the doer, the achiever - the one who recognizes the challenges and does something about it.
~ Vince Lombardi

Who Will You Serve?

There is no business in existence that came into being without answering the all important question of who they would serve. Being in service to others will be the most satisfying and rewarding life experience you will have, and will benefit you both personally and financially.

Think about your local grocer, the plumber, the clothing boutique, and the nail salon in your city. They each thrive on being of service to the people who seek groceries, plumbing repairs and upgrades, stylish and affordable clothing, and pedicures.

When new entrepreneurs first come to me they are often unable to answer this simple question regarding who they wish to serve, so this is typically where we begin. The follow up question, once you have answered this one is "what's for sale?" and can be just as confusing when you are first getting started. I'll address that part of entrepreneurial success in greater detail later in this book.

If you lead with "I just want to make money" then you have missed the point entirely. Can you imagine someone going through seven years of college to become a veterinarian with the goal of just wanting to make money? It was my dream for many years to become a veterinarian and I never gave more than a fleeting thought as to the financial aspects of this career. Instead, I thought about healing sick and injured animals, learning more about how to keep them healthy, and the joy we receive from animals of all kinds throughout our lifetime and theirs. I wanted to spend my days surrounded by creatures great and small who needed the human touch to restore them to full health.

It's the exact same thing in your business. Think about the people who will come to you as their trusted advisor for solutions to their problems and issues around the topic you have chosen to be an authority in as a part of your business. Once your mind shifts to this way of thinking your business will grow exponentially and will be limitless in proportion. The world will truly be your oyster.

Now you may be thinking that you aren't quite sure which types of problems you will be able to solve for people online. You may believe that you do not possess any specialized knowledge or information and that no one would seek you out as their trusted advisor. You may even have some valid (at least to your way of thinking right now) reasons and excuses as to why you will not succeed. These may include, but will not be limited to thinking that you are too old, too young, not smart enough, do not possess enough education, missing the right kind of education, don't have friends already doing this, do not have technical skills, do not have writing skills, and too many more to list here. Curious as to how I know this? Yes, that's correct, I had most of these limiting beliefs as well.

We all felt similarly and had this type of belief system when we were getting started as online entrepreneurs. I've spent time with some of the biggest names working online today and they have shared with me that they did not have a clue as to how they would serve others when they first came online. Then they had a mental shift and it all came together for them. Each of them shared experiences that were almost identical to mine, so I know there is something to what I have already shared and what I am about to tell you here.

When you get started with online marketing and entrepreneurship everything moves very quickly. You are exposed to a myriad of information and concepts unfamiliar to you, and soon you feel bogged down in the learning and implementing of tasks and activities that are confusing and time consuming and just plain difficult. You feel as though it will take a lifetime to get up to speed on everything you must know in order to be even a little bit successful as an online entrepreneur. And then it happens...

Someone from your "real" life asks you about what you are doing and you begin to explain it to them. It's awkward at first, and then you get going with your explanation and description and suddenly you realize that you have learned far more than you had previously thought. A surge of wonder and joy courses through your veins and you are truly excited to be sharing your knowledge and experience and expertise with this person. You look around, hoping that you have not let out a squeal of delight that could be heard by others. Yes, you realize at that moment you have knowledge and experience and expertise far above what the average person has, and that people now look up to you as their...are you ready for it? They look up to you as their trusted advisor.

This is the moment in time you were waiting for. As my own students go through this and share it with me and with the other members of our group I am in awe of what awaits them. Their confidence and self-esteem are at an all time high as they step into the shoes of what is to come.

Now is the time to choose who you will serve and to dedicate your business life to the pursuit of helping others to solve their problems and to attain their goals, based on what you can share with them. You will go on to create information products, write books, give presentations, host live events, and create membership sites around the topics you are becoming more and more of an expert in every single day.

And as a humble servant to others, your learning never stops. You will continue to read books, articles, and blog posts related to your niche. You will buy information products, take online courses, join membership sites, and engage in discussions around your topic, all in the hope that even more light will be shed upon the answers to questions and the solutions to problems that others are seeking. And at some moment in time you will see yourself quite differently than you ever have before. You have become an expert and an authority and serving others in this capacity has become your life's work and will be your legacy. You have arrived.

Be willing to do the work, take the time, and make the effort to arrive in style. Do whatever it takes every single day to move upward and onward in this way. And finally, after doing this for some period of time you will never be able to return to the thinking and the actions that once bogged you down. Instead of trudging through the mud you are floating in the clouds. I often say that my books mostly write themselves and that my fingers are guided over the keys to get just the right meaning out of my head and on to my readers. As I'm typing this I am having the exact experience you are reading about at this moment in time. I want this for you and will do whatever it takes to help you on your journey to inspired entrepreneurship. It is a special place that leads with your heart, mind, and spirit to bring you as close as possible to your goals and dreams. They are always just out of reach, because you will continue to set new ones for yourself. You see, you are serving yourself as much, if not more than you are serving others and this is as it should be.

Section Four

Getting an audience is hard.
Sustaining an audience is hard.
It demands a consistency of thought, of purpose,
and of action over a long period of time.
~ Bruce Springsteen

How Do You Do What It Takes?

The difference between knowing *what* to do and understanding *how* to do it can be compared to watching traffic go by in front of your house and driving across the country by yourself. One will make you proficient in the theory of driving in traffic and maneuvering around obstacles, while the other will give you a hands on experience not possible without actually having the experience on an internal level. You will find that many courses, products, trainings, and even books are filled with lots of the *what* you need to do, along with the theories behind it and very little, if any of the *how* you actually do it on your own to achieve the results you are after. This may be due in part to the fact that learning what to do makes you feel uplifted and hopeful, at least in the short run and learning how to do it can make you feel anxious and confused. I have a solution for this dilemma, and that is why I created this entrepreneurial playbook for you.

As you are learning what to do to build a profitable online business that will support your lifestyle, take small actions along the way. Instead of reading more and doing nothing, commit to trying what you learn, at least on a small scale. Allow me to give you an example.

Way back in 2006 when I was first getting started everyone was talking about blogging as the wave of the future. Blogs (this is short for web log) were fairly new on the scene at that time and seemed like an excellent way to get your information out to the world. Perhaps no one would actually see what you had posted unless you gave them the link, but just knowing it was there made a difference in your mind. You were a blogger, even if it was mostly a well guarded secret.

I had two choices that year. I could have continued to read and learn everything there was to know about blogs or I could jump in with both feet, start a blog, and begin writing. I chose the latter, and the rest is history.

Actually there is more to this story that I want to share with you. It was January of 2006 and I was at the crossroads between learning and doing. As a professional student during most of my adult years I was tempted to keep learning. But the emerging entrepreneur in me urged me to take action as well. The goal was to enhance my learning by actually taking action and experiencing what it was like to blog.

The previous year I had started a blog on one of the free platforms to show my fifth and sixth grade students what this technology was all about. I posted about our science fair projects and showed them around this new website. Encouraging them to embrace technology and new forms of expression was topmost in my mind, so I clicked around on the site to see what could be done. I added a picture and then resized it and moved it to the other side of the post. I added a page to introduce myself and then deleted it so I could start again. I changed the language from English to German, clicked around some more, and then the blog disappeared. Forever. Because I speak absolutely no German whatsoever I had inadvertently clicked to "löschen sie diesen Blog", which translates to "delete this blog" and the software simply followed my instructions. My students got a laugh out of this and I learned an important lesson - put more thought into your actions and your results will be more effective and long lasting..

So instead of poking around and continuing to be a novice in this world, that January I enrolled in an online training course on blogging. There were one hundred students in this virtual classroom and we each paid one hundred dollars for four months of training and a year's access to the forum and membership area. This turned out to be the best opportunity I could have hoped for and I took action while I was learning.

It was similar with every new piece of the online marketing puzzle I encountered over that next couple of years. When faced with the daunting task of writing sales copy for my information products I did purchase several books to learn as much as I could. But after a week or so of reading about what needed to be done I actually jumped in and began writing my own copy.

One method I used was to copy entire sales pages in long hand, a tedious task that was supposed to help me internalize the process and the formula so that it all made sense. I would position my computer so that I could see it from my writing desk, enabling me to write in long passages without adjusting my posture. Some of the web sales copy would translate into ten pages or more of written text. It wasn't long before I could feel the rhythm of how they unfolded the product within the sales copy and I knew intuitively what was coming next or if a section had been repositioned or deleted altogether. This practice has proved to be invaluable to me over these past ten years of creating and selling a variety of products in various niches online.

As I move through the steps and ideas and concepts of teaching you how you can start and grow a successful online business, be open to and willing to taking action at each juncture. Sometimes it will be exhausting and tedious, but only until you have done it a number of times. Remember that it's all about doing what it takes to make your dreams and goals come to life for you.

And go back to the beginning of this section to reread the quote I've included from musician Bruce Springsteen. Even he realized that marketing and relationship building was going to make the difference between his success and possible failure in the music business when he got started back in the 1970s. Interesting. And here I thought it was all about the music.

Chapter Twelve

Often the difference between a successful person
and a failure is not one has better abilities or ideas,
but the courage that one has to bet on one's ideas,
to take a calculated risk - and to act.
~ Maxwell Maltz

The Entrepreneur's Playbook

Here is where I will share a blueprint of sorts to get you started in the right direction. Earlier I stated that there will never be an exact blueprint for entrepreneurial success because of the very nature of what this entails. I stand by that statement, but with the caveat that you must never rely on a step by step strategy developed by someone else if you truly want to create something unique to your own needs and desires. So think of this blueprint more like a guideline for what is to come after you get started and your business is off the ground. I use the sports reference "playbook" in an attempt to share both the tactics and strategies of business, much as a sports team does when working closely with the players leading up to the next big game.

Also, remember that you may have a very different vision for what you want your business to look like from what someone else would envision and that excellence and success is always in the eyes of the beholder. With that said, let's get moving in the direction of your journey to entrepreneurial success.

My dream and prayer when I began my journey was to create a business I could run from home to earn enough income to pay all of my bills and financial obligations with grace and ease. This was based on my many years of working both as a classroom teacher and in real estate, and my experiences with illness and injury that caused me to lose time from work and endure financial hardship. Initially, I prayed for work I could do from my bedroom, if I were unable to leave my bedside.

I searched for over a year to discover something I could do that would satisfy my need to be able to work from my home. It was when I listened to an audio recording of a man who was selling eBooks on a variety of topics from homemade websites that the bright light turned on for me. This was what I wanted to learn more about and to develop for myself. I can still remember what it felt like as I listened to him describe this type of business. I must have played that CD fifty times in preparation for the journey I was so ready to embark upon.

I knew that I needed to do some research to figure out what information people were searching for, and then create, or have created for me, a product to sell to them. It would all be set up and delivered electronically, so I also needed a website, a payment processor, and a service to deliver my email messages over time to those who had purchased.

Remember that internet marketing was still in its infancy at this point and all of these systems and processes were being tested and refined. I was to become a pioneer and this was simultaneously frightening and exhilarating.

In its simplicity, the tactical pieces of your entrepreneurial playbook will consist of these key items:
- ✓ A hosted WordPress website
- ✓ An autoresponder service
- ✓ A payment processing service
- ✓ Access to a word processing program
- ✓ Products to promote through your affiliate link
- ✓ Your own products and services

We use WordPress because it has become the most powerful CMS (content management system) available anywhere. It must be hosted so that you own and control the sites you develop over time. To date, I have more than three hundred of these WordPress sites.

There are several free blogging and website platforms available on the internet. Avoid these at all costs! When you do not own and control a site it might disappear at any time. One example of this is Squidoo, a platform many of us used regularly to publish simple websites to sell products, share information, rank for our keywords, and promote our other sites. I even taught an online course on how to best utilize this site for your business. Then one day in 2014 it was announced that the site would be shutting down forever, leaving millions of people who had built businesses exclusively using Squidoo's platform out in the cold. Let this experience serve as an example and a warning of just what can happen when you depend on free services to build your business.

An autoresponder service is necessary so that you may communicate with your prospects and clients through a series of email messages. My recommendations for this are located within the Resources section at the end of this book.

I was confused as to the difference between autoresponders and broadcasts when I was first starting my business. An autoresponder message is written in advance and sent out to people automatically when they opt in to your list, purchase a product, or take another action that sets the process in motion. A broadcast message is written and sent out in real time, and typically contains time sensitive information. Strategic use of both autoresponder emails and broadcasts is crucial to your success as an entrepreneur.

Processing payments becomes important once you have your own product or service to sell to others. Again, my recommendations for this are in the Resources section. Keep it simple in the beginning, and then graduate on to a more sophisticated method as your business grows. Companies are more open to serving home based businesses these days, so you can thank the online marketing pioneers of the late 1990s and early 2000s for that.

Word processing programs are necessary for everything we write, both in our personal and professional lives. There are free programs available, but you already know how I feel about that strategy. Don't put unnecessary limitations on your business growth in order to save a few dollars. Instead, budget for what you need, if you don't have it already. Almost on a daily basis I need to be able to create written documents and presentations that will look and feel professional to the people I am serving.

Affiliate marketing is a topic unto itself, and I would highly recommend you read my popular book on this topic. Suffice it to say that you will have an unlimited inventory of products and services to recommend to others this way, and by only recommending what and who you know and have benefited from your reputation will grow in the most positive way over time. You are welcome to become my affiliate if this is a good fit for you. Again, information on how to do this can be found at the end of this book in the Resources section.

Finally, you will become an information product creator. The idea is that you will create digital products on niche topics to sell to people who are in need of this information. I go into greater detail on this in the following chapter, but it doesn't hurt to read this more than once. The products you will create and sell will:

1) Answer people's questions
2) Help solve their problems
3) Alleviate some of their pain

Here is an excellent example of what I am talking about here.

Back in 2007, when I had been in business for less than a year, a man in my Rotary Club was telling me about his dog. I have several dogs and have always been a dog lover, so I believe he knew that I would be interested in his story.

His family pet had contracted cancer and was not expected to live much longer. He told me that he just wanted to know what to expect, how to make the dog as comfortable as possible, and to help himself and his family members to feel a little better during these final days.

I told him that I understood, having lost my basset hound, Abigail to stomach cancer just two years earlier.

And then he told me something so amazing that I could hardly believe my ears. He and his wife had searched online for information about this and had found an eBook on the topic of cancer in dogs.

I asked him if this book promised to cure their dog's cancer and his answer was no, of course not.

"Then why did you buy it?" I asked.

"Because it made us feel so much better and gave us some valuable information and insight about what we were going through.

And it made us think about the situation in a way that comforted us and made sense to my family."

And then he said something that really got my attention.

"And it was only forty dollars."

I had spent the previous year believing that people would not pay more than ten dollars for information of this type, and that only topics like real estate could warrant higher prices. It was a story I was telling myself and had no basis in truth. This information product had great value to this man and his family in that it answered their questions, helped to solve their problem, and had alleviated some of the pain they were going through in their lives.

Choose a niche or niches that you know well and are willing to spend time in sharing with others. My very first information product was an eBook on real estate farming.

If you are not familiar with this phrase, "farming" refers to the process of staking a claim in a specific area of your town and then staying in contact with its residents. Knocking on doors to introduce yourself, using a reverse phone directory to call people, and mailing notepads and other small gifts are all ways to farm your area. This is all done in hopes of obtaining listings and securing other transactions with the people you are connecting with. After working for more than twenty years in real estate I had this part of the job down cold, making me something of an expert on the topic.

You may also wish to provide services to your target audience to start earning some income more quickly. As soon as I could install and set up WordPress sites within fifteen minutes, I began to offer this as a service to others. They would come in through my affiliate link for the hosting service, and I would set up their site as a bonus. I earned sixty-five dollars each time, and if you do the math you'll find that two hundred sixty dollars for an hour of my time was well worth it at the beginning of my career as an online entrepreneur.

What I have outlined here is simply the tactics of your playbook and blueprint. While this is important, it is the strategies that make it all come alive. The next chapter is where I discuss that part in greater detail as I explain the three-pronged strategy that has helped my business to continue to grow exponentially over these past ten years.

Chapter Thirteen

Life is too short to waste.
Dreams are fulfilled only through action,
not through endless planning to take action.
~ David J. Schwartz

Your Three-Pronged Strategy

Now your entrepreneurial playbook will really take off when you learn and implement the strategies I include in this chapter. When I finally got my momentum in my online business I decided to create what I refer to as a three-pronged strategy for building and growing steadily and consistently over time. These are the three prongs:

- ✓ Content Creation and Syndication
- ✓ Product Creation/Selection/Distribution
- ✓ Massive Marketing

I will go into great detail about each one here so that you can get a better idea of what online entrepreneurship entails on a daily basis. This will never be a "set it and forget it" business, or one that runs on autopilot. In fact, you would not even want to get involved with something that makes those kinds of promises. Why? Because then anyone could do it and you wouldn't be able to maximize your results by doing what it takes. There is no "easy button" in life or business, only strategies, techniques, and methods based on experience and hard work that will eventually feel like child's play to you if you keep at it for a long enough time. That's why you will study my strategies I am presenting as a part of the entrepreneur's playbook and then make the changes to each piece of the puzzle over time to transform it into a system that will be uniquely your own.

Content Creation and Syndication

What used to be the most difficult and challenging part of my business now comes easily to me because I disciplined myself to get into the habit of writing every day. I've become a content creation machine over these past ten years, publishing and syndicating various types of content in an unending stream throughout cyberspace.

This did not come easily to me during my first months as an online entrepreneur. I had been the person who wanted so desperately to be a writer yet did very little actual writing. I would enroll in a creative writing course and then wait until the very end to get my assignments completed. I loved the idea of *having written* much more than the actual process of writing.

This all changed when I came online. Very quickly I realized that I had to start creating content every day to get a foothold in my niche. I put my head down and got to work. It was a painful process in the beginning, but soon I got into the habit of writing every day and the words began to flow. And remember that content may also be in the formats of recordings and videos, so it is not limited to just the written word.

Think of content as the glue that holds your business together and makes it run 24/7/365, no matter where you are and what you are doing. For example, I may write a blog post one day and leave for a trip the next, yet that content continues to serve and represent me as it travels through cyberspace and connects with people all over the world. Push as much quality, relevant content out to the world in the form of written, audio, and video information and you will be handsomely rewarded for years to come.

Once you publish something on the internet it's almost impossible to get rid of it. This has both positive and negative consequences. If it's something you no longer want people to see it can be pushed back a few hundred spots in a Google search, but it is still there. It's similar to deleting something off the hard drive on your computer; you can do that but it is still in the recesses of the hardware and accessible by someone who knows how to locate it. So think about what you write and say before you do it and you will be fine.

The positive side of this discussion is that once you publish something people searching by keyword are always likely to find it. From experience I will tell you to only use domains you intend to keep forever, as once you give up a domain you had published under then eventually someone else will be able to snatch it up for a few dollars. We all learn this the hard way in the beginning so that's why I am mentioning it here.

Product Creation/Selection/Distribution

This is actually three things in one, so let's begin with a discussion of information products. First of all, what exactly *is* an information product? I describe it as being:

Information on a topic of interest at a given time to a segment of the population that will answer their questions, solve their problems, and alleviate their pain. It will be delivered digitally and in a variety of formats. Remember these three criteria, as addressing them gives you the keys to the kingdom when it comes to information product creation. I will mention them again and again to reinforce their importance in this process of digital product creation.

In the previous chapter I have discussed the topic of information products as well, but it doesn't hurt to provide you with even more examples in this chapter.

These products may originate from someone's ideas or life experiences, or be curated from materials already available on the topic in question. The ideal information product spares the prospect from the grueling process of seemingly endless research, analysis, and summary and boils it all down into an easily consumable format. Here are some examples that will be helpful to you in understanding this part of your playbook.

Years ago a product was released on how to use YouTube most effectively and efficiently. I knew the two product creators well and purchased the training right away to learn as much as I could. When I saw one of them at a marketing conference where we were both speaking soon after it was released, I asked him how he and his partner were able to put together such a massive amount of information, with such great detail and examples. His answer astounded me.

"We used YouTube's information and broke it down so that everyone could understand and utilize it to their advantage."

They had created an excellent product simply by Googling for the information and presenting it in an entirely different light. Yes, this is perfectly acceptable and many companies welcome and even encourage this type of synthesization of their original ideas and innovations. It's a win-win scenario. It is not plagiarism, lest you think I am condoning the stealing of someone's intellectual property or content. Instead, think of it as a review, where you give full credit and attribution to the original author(s) and completely rewrite all of the material you wish to sell.

Now you must first begin by doing the research to see if the product or product line you wish to create is a financially viable one. Make sure this information is not already available at no cost, in an easily digestible format. In the case of my example above, even though YouTube provides everything you need for free, it doesn't mean that the layperson will be able to decipher it and add it to their repertoire of knowledge. I had looked through YouTube's trainings on many occasions and had given up each time because the language was way over my head for this topic. There is gold in explaining material that is, or is perceived to be highly technical in nature, somewhat confusing, or that contains ambiguous information.

Start small, and then gear up to create information products on a regular basis. Currently I have about fifty of these types of products, and I am regularly creating new ones in a variety of ways. Many are from my original ideas and experiences, others originate as private label rights content that was researched and prepared in full before I purchased it and repurposed it, and others from information already available online and repurposed for easy consumption.

Some of the very best information products come from a combination of sources. That was the case when I created my Really Simple Podcasting training course during the fall of 2015.

Even though I had been podcasting successfully for over four years, I had outsourced the technical pieces and actually knew very little as to how it all came together over at iTunes. Many people, including my own students began asking me for more information on how they could start podcasting without having to take on the expense of having technical help. So I decided to do some detailed research, share my own experiences, and include some excellent PLR (private label rights) content to flesh it out as a definitive resource on this topic. This product continues to be an extremely popular one that has helped hundreds of people get their podcasts up and running.

And information products have long since gone mainstream, lest you think your products must relate to online marketing or technology. I can remember when a friend of mine showed up at a charity dinner with a legal sized manila folder under her arm. She proudly turned it over to me so I could see the eBook she had purchased online and subsequently printed out. The topic was "restless legs syndrome", something she had struggled with for years. I couldn't believe my eyes, as this was someone who detested the internet and all it had to offer. When I asked her about this, she explained that she just couldn't take the pain and discomfort any longer and had searched online the night before to find some answers. The result was her purchasing the eBook for twenty-seven dollars and being very happy with the results so far. Could she have found most, if not all of this information herself? Yes, of course, but she wanted answers to her questions, a solution to her problem, and to have at least some of her physical pain alleviated quickly, so this just made more sense.

Also, create products that will require minimal research on your part in the beginning. Make a list of the topics you know well, based on your life experiences. Then create a short outline of what you could include in a product on this topic. I began in the area of real estate because I had already been involved with it for more than twenty years when I came online. I mentioned this earlier in the book.

I had a new neighbor who showed up at my door in tears one day. She and her husband had had a huge argument about money, and he had told her she had to get a "real" job and give up real estate because she just wasn't earning enough income. She was bringing in so little business at the time and it was still taking up all of her waking hours. We discussed how she found prospects and it turned out she knew very little about something called "farming".

Farming is the process of choosing a geographical area in your city to focus on and serve. Over time it pays off handsomely as more and more people get to know you. It includes calling people on the phone, sending out postcards, newsletters, and other useful material, and actually knocking on doors to meet people in person. I had been very good at this marketing strategy and used to farm several areas successfully. It got to the point where I could do this with minimal time and effort for maximum results and payoff.

I began to share some of my strategies and experiences with my neighbor, and then decided to write it all down. The result was an eBook I sold on a website for forty-seven dollars. This was my very first information product and I updated it regularly until finally taking it off the market a few years later. During that time I sold more than a thousand copies, making this one of the wisest decisions I made during my early entrepreneurial career. And my neighbor began to get listings and make sales based on what she had learned from me, making a "real" job unnecessary. Her testimonial was one of the most heartfelt I have ever received and I was proud to share it on the sales page for that product.

And this eBook was far from perfect! I edited and updated it regularly during the time I had it for sale. Digital information products lend themselves to this kind of scrutiny because updating the file and making sure previous buyers get access to the revised edition is one of the simplest things you will ever do.

I think of "product selection" as referring to the many affiliate products I recommend regularly. Because you will have access to literally thousands of digital products, you must go through the selection process carefully before something makes the cut. I purchase products and courses almost daily, yet only about a dozen fall into the category of being something I loved, benefitted from, and now wish to recommend.

The more selective you are the more people will trust you to only tell them about the very best products, and this is a reputation you want to enhance over time. Now people will email me to ask my opinion before purchasing, and this brings me additional income as I am honest in my replies. It starts a conversation that will save them time and money, as well as getting them closer to the goals they wish to achieve.

"Product distribution" is the term I use to describe the process in which I choose physical products to sell on Amazon and other sites. This is a relatively new business model for me that I got started with in late 2013. I had taken a course on this topic and was determined to give it a try.

Starting with private label products was not the best strategy for me, as I was in way over my head from the very beginning. I put that aside for a few months to jump into retail arbitrage, and that was a wise move on my part. I learned so much that I could then apply to my own products in order to make more sales. Finally I started wholesaling products, and my profits went up dramatically as I learned more and made better decisions. As with all things in business, staying the course and learning as much as possible will always be beneficial in the long run.

I'm not going to share any more about this business model with you here, as this entrepreneur's playbook relates more to digital products. I have provided some valuable resources with you at the end of the book if you want to pursue this further.

Massive Marketing

I am now stuck with the moniker "Marketing Mad Woman" and I wear this hat with immense pride. It turns out that marketing is what makes you money and keeps you in business. It's the glue that makes everything stick. I continue to say that if I had known more about marketing while I was in real estate, everything would have been easier and run more smoothly for me. Marketing must be a daily process in whatever you are involved with in your business. Back in those days I just didn't understand this principle. Instead, I gave up any marketing efforts as soon as I had a client, only to have long dry spells when my marketing had to once again catch up with my demand for new business.

There was a real estate agent named Jerry (I won't use his last name here) who marketed like crazy during my years as a real estate broker and residential appraiser. His tag line was "Call Jerry and start packing!" I thought he was so silly and that what he was doing was such a waste of time. He engaged in every type of advertising available back then - this was before social media - and was always finding new ways to get his name in front of prospects. If I had paid attention to his methods and incorporated even a few of them into my own business, things would have been much different for me. I Googled him just before writing this section and he is still going strong. Good for Jerry for doing what it takes to set himself apart from almost everyone else in his geographical area.

So let's get back to discussing what you need to do for your online business. Marketing on the internet has never been simpler, at least from my perspective. I can sit in front of my computer and get my message out to the world with just a few keystrokes. Most of the marketing I do is free, and even the paid advertising is not that expensive if you consider the return on your investment.

Every morning I start my day by thinking about what I could do to market myself and my business in a new and innovative way. I don't always come up with an earth shattering new strategy, but I do take action with whatever ideas come up for me.

One of my best ideas was to create a post I could add to regularly, and then purchase a domain forwarded to that post. The most relevant example I will share with you here is ProductivityChallenge2016.com. I've hosted a productivity challenge every spring since 2011. Some were for twenty-one days, but I prefer to go for thirty days for best results. Every day I add something to the post, and then people read it and leave a comment on what they think, the questions they have, and how they are taking action with what I am sharing there.

The result is massive traffic to my website, people connecting with each other, a five to six thousand word post (massive content), and a new free product I can use as a giveaway or a short report. I monetize this by including relevant links to my own or affiliate products and to my mentoring programs. It takes me about fifteen minutes a day for each of the thirty days, and that is to write something new and to approve and reply to the comments. I highly recommend this, no matter what you niche.

In the Appendix at the end of this book I have included the complete transcript of my most recent Productivity Challenge. Read through it carefully and see how, in addition to helping the audience

I serve, it continues to get my message and my expertise out to the world.

And try not to think of marketing as a chore. Have fun with it and you will reap the rewards. It turns out this is an area where I excel, and I actually look forward to the marketing of anything I want to share with others. I have found over these years that the overwhelming majority of people prefer to write, create products, and even do technology rather than to market their products and services on the internet. So much potential income is left on the table with this thinking, so don't allow it to happen to you.

Chapter Fourteen

In a crowded marketplace, fitting in is a failure.
In a busy marketplace, not standing
out is the same as being invisible.
~ Seth Godin

Establishing Credibility and Visibility

In the "real" world we have all grown up in, credibility was established the old fashioned way; you earned it over a period of time; a very long period of time. Today that is only part of the picture, as we have the ability to build up our credibility much more quickly and in very creative ways with the advent of the internet and the speed at which technology is progressing.

Now in real estate, the word "creative" is used to describe alternative ways to finance a property so that someone who would not be able to qualify for a loan is still able to purchase property. This is a commonly accepted type of transaction these days. Think of this in a similar way on the internet.

I needed to establish my credibility quickly when I came online during 2006. If I had known then what I know now (that famous phrase) then I would have started blogging, interviewed thought leaders, created information products, and written and published a book during my very first year. But I had to start from where I was at that time in my life and with what I knew, so blogging was all I could think of back then.

Also, my confidence level was not very high and my self esteem was at an all time low, so starting from that point made it like slogging my way through mud filled with debris. Even so, I was willing to do whatever it would take to achieve my goals.

But you do not have to suffer and endure such hardship, as you are here, during 2016 or shortly thereafter, and will have the full benefit of my experience when it comes to building your credibility to get your business off the ground more quickly. This is exactly what I recommend for my high level clients in one of my Mentor programs. Let's go deeper now into the areas of building credibility and increasing your visibility on the internet.

Building Your Credibility

Once you have determined the niche you will be working in, start a blog and begin posting with regularity. I define this as a minimum of twice a week during your first year online and at least once a week thereafter. I often joke that you do not need to do this forever, only until you die! Finding your voice is key here, and that may take you some time. Writing every day during your "prime time" hours will allow your inner voice to finally speak its mind. Once you begin to look forward to this time to write you will have found your voice and the words will flow naturally, as if inspired. You want your topic to be broad enough to garner general interest, yet narrow enough to set you apart from everyone else.

For example, I have a very smart client right now who has been blogging about marketing in general and local business marketing more specifically. The problem is that general marketing is way too broad for most of the people she would like to reach, and local business marketing is now much more common than it has been in recent years. My advice to her was that she share her own story of how she started her business more than twenty years ago and climbed her way up the ladder of success, despite having some serious challenges and setbacks along the way.

Building your credibility through regular blogging allows you the opportunity to have what is known as an "authority site" under your control. You want your blog to be found regularly through keyword searches for your topic, and to be the stopping off place for anyone who needs more information on your topic. By writing and publishing to your site on a regular basis you will train the search engines to index your site and share it in their results for your keyword phrases.

Remember that people are at different levels when they find you, and that most people will arrive at your site through a side door, meaning they will be led to a specific post on your blog rather than to the front page of your site. Make sure they know who you are from the second they arrive and that you have enough information on your "About" page to warrant their remaining to read and learn more about you, as well as to join your list and begin hearing from you regularly. This strategy will serve you well over time.

Storytelling

Using storytelling to get people's attention is an excellent method for building up your credibility. These stories come from what you are willing to share with others, so only share what you are comfortable with in regards to your personal life. People who know of me have heard my story of working as a classroom teacher for twenty years, while also working in real estate as a broker and residential appraiser. I speak of being exhausted from my seven days a week schedule and rethinking it all after being diagnosed with cancer and suffering a serious work injury while at school.

This part is what I refer to as my "before" story.

I made the conscious decision to leave it all behind, and by 2006 I had resigned from the school district, given away my real estate clients, and started my online business as a new entrepreneur. It was a steep learning curve as I began to blog when I wasn't a writer, and to set up web pages when I wasn't very technical. Soon I began to earn some money and was hopeful that I could replace my previous income over time.

This is my "after" story. But it doesn't end there...

Within a year and a half I had replaced my previous income and was moving beyond that point. My writing had improved dramatically and I had already written more than two hundred articles and blog posts. Everything was easier because I now had some real world experience, and I had created several products and started a mentor program for others who wanted to emulate what I had achieved.

This is what is called an "after *after*" story.

Do you see the flow of this? Share your story of where you came from, what you were able to achieve, and how that has grown over time. The "before after *after*" three part story is the most powerful one you can share because everyone wants to know what is possible in the future.

I am positive that I earn more income than many others as a result of my rich storytelling style. No matter where I am in the world and what I am doing I choose to share the details in a way that almost always comes back to my business. This is an art that anyone can learn with practice, yet it continues to be my observation that few engage in storytelling in such a way.

Becoming a Published Author

Writing and publishing my first book, *Huge Profits With a Tiny List: How to Use Relationship Marketing to Increase Your Bottom Line*, changed everything for me in terms of how credible I was in the eyes of the world.

I can remember being at Armand Morin's huge marketing conference in Minneapolis, Minnesota in the spring of 2010 about to go on stage to present, when I received a call from another well known marketer. He wanted me to speak at his event that coming September, and while we were talking he asked to confirm that indeed, my book would be published within the next few months. He told me he only wanted published authors speaking at his event so that it would be perceived in a way that would behoove all of us. I was able to confidently let him know the book was scheduled for release within the next six weeks and that I would be thrilled to accept his offer of this speaking engagement.

When I was introduced at this event it was as "a published author" and that gave me instant credibility.

For this first book I had blogged each chapter, or at least the ideas and information for each chapter. I did this with fifty blog posts and then did a copy and paste of each of them into my word processing document. You can do the same exact thing if that will be easier for you.

I have an entire book and an online course on the topic of writing and publishing your book - *Write. Publish. Prosper. How to Write Prolifically, Publish Globally, and Prosper Eternally* - so I won't say anything more about it here other than to strongly encourage you to write and publish your first book sooner rather than later for maximum credibility in your chosen niche.

In the offline world it can take as long as a quarter of a century to build up the credibility needed to position yourself as an expert in your field. Notice that I said *an* expert, not *the* expert. There is a difference. *An* expert can be one of many, while *the* expert is assumed to stand alone at the apex and pinnacle of their career. Being an expert and an authority in your area is achievable in as little as ninety days when you utilize all of the strategies, methods, and techniques I am teaching and sharing with you here.

Increasing Your Visibility

Visibility is being "everywhere" on the internet. When someone purchases one of my books, information products, or courses I like to ask them where they first heard about me. Sometimes they have heard me speak at a live event, listened to one of my podcasts, or read my blog. But the most common answer and the one I like hearing the most is that I was "everywhere" online when they were searching for information on one of the topics I have come to be known for. This is the goal you are striving for in your own business as an entrepreneur. You can best achieve this through social media, content syndication, and media exposure and publicity.

Social Media

I started online during the Dark Ages. There was no social media. I'll pause for a second while you catch your breath and regain your composure. That's right, we were all alone behind our computers, hoping that the ideas would come and that we could figure it all out. And most importantly, that somebody somewhere in the world would find us and let us know.

Of course, there were forums and bulletin boards, but they were populated with people who were either very technical or very academic. I can remember visiting some of those sites back in the day and asking my simple questions. I got answers, but not the ones I was hoping for. Sometimes I couldn't even understand the answer they gave to my question, so I soon gave up and looked for other means of communication.

If I had purchased a product or training from someone I would often email them with my questions, and typically within a day or two I would hear back with an answer. But it was all very impersonal and you had to have great patience to endure this style of learning.

By the end of 2007 and into 2008 two things occurred that would change the internet forever. The first was Facebook opening its site up to the general public. Before that time you needed to be a student or faculty member at a college or university and have an email account from your school in order to open up and maintain a Facebook account.

The second was the creation of even more social media sites, namely Twitter. In the early days you could actually have conversations with people on Twitter in real time, but as the number of users increased exponentially it changed from being personal to being more of a site for sharing your news, updates, and more.

LinkedIn had already established itself as a site for people in the corporate world to connect and seek out jobs, assignments, and projects, but they felt the pressure from Facebook, I believe, and became more social in nature. I have a reach of almost thirty million people on six continents because of my slow, steady, methodical approach to increasing my visibility in this way.

My motto for all social media is to "get in, get out, and get back to work" and this has served me well over the years. Plan on spending about thirty minutes every other day on all social media, and this will enable you to share your blog posts, products, thoughts, ideas, and more while not detracting from the actual work required to build your business.

And remember that storytelling is just as important here. We all listen and tune in to stories, no matter in which format they are presented to us. Social media is built on sharing stories, even if only a hundred or so characters at a time on Twitter or with a picture, inforgraphic, video, or quote on Facebook or LinkedIn.

Content Syndication

If you are old enough to remember Ann Landers and her advice column you know that she was from Chicago, Illinois and began by writing for the Chicago Sun-Times in 1943. Actually, the name *Ann Landers* was a pen name created by Chicago Sun-Times writer Ruth Crowley in 1943. It was taken over by Esther Pauline "Eppie" Lederer in 1955 and that's when the full syndication began. Instead of her column only being available to those living in the Chicago metropolitan area and having access to the Sun-Times, the newspaper reached an agreement with twenty-six other newspapers across the country who would also carry it. I was a teenager living in Miami when I first started reading her column in *The Miami Herald* circa 1968, and later on when I returned to California I picked up where I had left off by reading her column in the *Los Angeles Times*.

Content syndication is a beautiful thing, in that we can write or record or film something locally and then share it globally through a variety of distribution channels. I start with social media sites such as the "Big Three" I named above, namely Facebook, Twitter, and LinkedIn. A site called Just Retweet helps to get the word out for your blog posts very effectively. I also use my Channel on YouTube to let the world know where I am and what I am doing.

Media Exposure and Publicity

I come from the school of "there is no such thing as bad publicity" and have enjoyed the perceived power and results that come from strategic and regular media exposure.

This was all new to me when I first came online, and I thought you still sent a facsimile (fax) to the editor of the local newspaper if you wanted to have something newsworthy published there. It turned out those days had already been long gone when I appeared on the scene. I was doing publicity and marketing for my Rotary Club at that time and decided this would be an excellent way to learn how everything worked so I could apply it to my own business.

After a series of blunders, it was a woman named Pat Willett who came to my rescue. She had been the media liaison for the largest school district in Santa Clarita, one of the towns I live in, for many years. She was also active in Zonta, a non-profit whose mission is to advance the status of women worldwide.

Pat was friendly and patient and showed me the ropes of using publicity to get the word out to the world about projects, events, and happenings. It's not surprising that I became a Zontian soon after connecting with Pat. She and her husband are also involved in another project near and dear to my heart, that of hosting exchange students, but that is a story for another day.

It turned out that press releases had gone online, and there are several ways to send them so that the right people find the information you want to share readily. Start with the free ones so you can get a feel for how and what to write. For example, all press releases are written in third person, so I would say "Connie Ragen Green announces her sixth annual Productivity Challenge" instead of using "I" to announce it.

The "Kindergarten Effect" is how I describe this aspect of marketing. If you've been around a kindergartener or remember being one yourself you know they will jump up and down and squeal with laughter at the smallest things. I like to tell the story of a Kindergarten student who could not wait to share his day with his family. While they sat anxiously awaiting a story of a science experiment or of learning to read new words, they instead were treated to his reenactment of how a fly had come into the classroom through an open window and landed on another student's arm! We all need to do more of that for our own businesses. Things we take for granted, like blogging or growing an email list are huge in the eyes of people who are not familiar with our world. Share the details of what you are doing by sending a press release once a month.

Your publicity and media exposure efforts will be enhanced and accelerated if you work at becoming what I refer to as a "local celebrity" in your city or town. I did this quite by accident in Santa Clarita, where I was living exclusively when I started my online business. When I began living simultaneously in Santa Barbara four years ago I worked on this in a more strategic and well thought out way.

In either city I am not able to connect with the thought leaders and other "movers and shakers" when I want to share something I am doing with other residents and groups with my town.

Offer to write a column for the local newspapers and magazines, be a guest on the radio shows, and offer to speak for local groups and organizations. All of these efforts will pay off handsomely over time.

Chapter Fifteen

When in doubt, make a fool of yourself.
There is a microscopically thin line between being
brilliantly creative and acting like the most gigantic idiot
on earth. So what the hell, leap.
~ Cynthia Heimel

The "Really Simple" Series

Branding is an area I am not an expert in, except to the extent I have done it within my own business since 2006. The truth is that online entrepreneurs need to brand themselves first and foremost, because we are the face and the integrity of our business. But in addition to that, we need to have a brand people can relate to.

I started with my "huge profits with a tiny list" brand. One of my two main blogs is titled with that, it was the title of my first published book, and this was the first topic I was asked to speak about at marketing events. My target audience resonated with the message that anyone could earn a huge profit with even a very tiny list of prospects and clients. The key factor is in how responsive that list is to hearing from you and taking action on your suggestions and recommendations.

However, this branding could have very well backfired if I hadn't been open to making a change years back. Many people are so new to online entrepreneurship they are not even familiar with what a "list" refers to, and the idea of making huge profits when just getting started may seem too far-fetched for them to fully comprehend.

Over the years I have branded various phrases, including my series of domains and products using the words "jump start". None of these seemed to stick in the way I was hoping for so I continued to test out new ones. But during 2015 I decided to start my "Really Simple" line of products and training courses and this strategy continues to be a winning one. Here is what I have created so far:

- ✓ Really Simple Podcasting
- ✓ Really Simple Content Marketing
- ✓ Really Simple Affiliate Marketing
- ✓ Really Simple Info Products
- ✓ Really Simple List Building
- ✓ Really Simple Plugins
- ✓ Really Simple Online Marketing
- ✓ Really Simple Membership Sites

My original goal was to create eight training courses and products during 2016. However, it appears that I moved too quickly and caused some confusion in the marketplace. My revised plan included reducing that number accordingly. I've been on fire in terms of creative energy and productivity, but sometimes the fire hose approach can be detrimental in the overall big picture and scheme of things.

Also, each of these information products is created and delivered in a slightly different manner. For example, my Really Simple Podcasting course was created based on my own experiences with producing two popular podcasts over the past four and a half years, as well as including some extremely well written PLR (private label rights) content that goes into greater technical detail than I would have been able to provide. I use the JV Zoo platform to sell this product, which means that I pay them a fee in order to have exposure to more affiliates. It continues to be a valuable experiment in my business strategy, and it definitely got my "Really Simple" branding in front of more people than I could have done on my own.

The other products are all on Nanacast, the platform I have used for almost five years to sell my products and run my affiliate program. This continues to be an effective system for running my business and I will continue in this way until there is a reason to initiate a change.

The "Really Simple" courses on content marketing, affiliate

marketing, and creating information products were all delivered first as live, interactive trainings in a virtual setting, and then made available as audio and video replays through a member's area. I then teach them live for a second and sometimes even a third time, allowing even more people to learn through this type of experience.

At some point in my experience of teaching courses online I began calling the first set of sessions "Season One" and when I hosted it live the next time I called it "Season Two" and so forth. This caught on quickly and now people look forward to my upcoming "seasons". I guess it's the show business connection that resonates with my community.

Really Simple Online Marketing is the "hub" site for all of these programs. This eliminates much of the confusion and gives people the opportunity to decide which of my trainings best fits their needs at the current time.

There is no right or wrong way to approach any of this, as it will depend upon what you are working to achieve and how you wish to deliver your information. So my advice to you would be to try out several things until you find the one that works best for you, and even then be flexible and open to change and trying something you have not done before. Do not ever try to get it perfect, but instead strive for excellence in everything you do. You have already read my thoughts on this topic earlier in the book.

Remember that you are your brand, and continue to get your name out in front of as many people as possible to best deliver your message to those who will only be able to hear it from you because of your unique gifts and talents.

Summary/Conclusion

> The most difficult thing is the decision to act,
> the rest is merely tenacity.
> ~ Amelia Earhart

You now have the tools you need to move forward in a positive and productive way as an online entrepreneur. You understand that doing what it takes will make all of the difference in the level of success you will achieve. And most importantly, you believe that you can and will make steady progress once you decide what you want and work towards that goal every single day. Just as this book did not write itself, no business has ever prospered without daily efforts from its creators.

Even though your reaction to reading much of what I have shared with you here may have prompted the three most dangerous words and thoughts known to man - "I know that" - resist the urge to not ask yourself the follow up question - "But am I doing it?" before moving on to other books and materials and seeking different answers to the same questions you have on how to start and build a lucrative online business.

Now that I have worked with hundreds of people in intimate business relationships and settings and thousands more through my group programs, at live events and in conferences, as well as over the internet I know that many people are looking for those different answers to the same questions. That is, they choose not to heed the advice offered by me and so many others to take action, course correct, and then take greater action. They seek an "easy button" that does not and should not exist when it comes to creating a lifestyle of time and financial freedom. Don't be like these people, because they are destined to go in circles and never prosper.

My example comes from the year 2010, when my mentors and other influential people on my life suggested I write a book. My first thought was that I could not possibly write a book. My reasons included not feeling like I was an expert in any area, not having the time, and not knowing how to get started. But by then I had learned to trust these people I had purposely surrounded myself with, and to heed their advice immediately.

I took a look at my blog posts and thought I could repurpose them into a book. This started with ten posts on how I was using "relationship marketing" to increase my income, even though my list was small. Over the next few weeks I added more posts of the ways I was able to do this, and then started a word processing document that included all of the relevant posts.

Course correction was necessary at every turn because I had created a big mess of information that wasn't tied together by a single thread. I reworked the content, turned some of it into a short report, and finally saw how I could divide my writing into chapters that would make sense to the reader.

Four months later the result was the release of *Huge Profits With a Tiny List: 50 Ways to Use Relationship Marketing to Increase Your Bottom Line*. The book wasn't perfect, and that's why I was able to do so well with it at that time. Readers saw the value in my ideas and knew that my goal was to strive for excellence rather than demand perfection.

My willingness to take action, course correct, and then take even greater action turned me into a published author. This led to speaking engagements, increased attendance for my virtual trainings, and finally bestseller status as more books sold.

Doing what it takes is a concept you will need to address on a daily basis until it becomes a habit. And know that all of us can slip back to the place where we were once upon a time when the right circumstances present themselves. After all of these years of working each day to boost my confidence and be a leader, occasionally I too fall from grace and again feel like a helpless child.

I am reminded of a time in 2012 when I was to speak at a larger marketing conference in Atlanta. One of my clients, someone whom I had not yet met in person offered to meet me at the car rental counter at Hartsfield-Jackson airport. We would be arriving by the early afternoon, and by the time he rented the car and we drove over to the hotel it would be in enough time to check into our rooms and meet others in the lobby to make our dinner arrangements.

Both of our flights ended up arriving several hours late, he was only able to rent a sub-compact car, and as we were driving away from the airport I asked him if he knew how to get to the hotel.

"I have no idea which way to go." he replied.

I quickly went into panic mode, and the thought of being in a city I did not know well, late at night, in a tiny car was all too much for me. When we saw a sign just minutes later that read "Take the next exit for Nashville, Tennessee" it was the last straw. As this was happening I thought about all the work I had done over the years to avoid feeling this way ever again, and it was an excellent reminder that the person we used to be will continue to live deep inside of us for the remainder of our lives.

Sitting up straight and tall in the passenger seat, I took out my phone and called the hotel. I told them exactly where we were and they got us turned around in the right direction. One wrong turn had thrown us off course, and the course correction was simple, fast, and painless. By the time we arrived at the hotel I had composed myself and filed this experience in my mind as one to remember and to learn from.

People often say to me that it must be great to work from home and do anything I want to at any time of the day. I answer them honestly when I say that I have never led a more structured, time managed life than I have since coming online. Everything I do each day is well thought out and planned. Yes, I am able to time-shift so that I can be available to do things on other people's schedules, but now that I am in the habit and flow of writing every morning, creating courses and products towards the middle of the day, and teaching during the late afternoon I know that this schedule works exceptionally well for me. Find your rhythm and turn it into a habit. You'll be glad you did.

Now go back and skim through this book (assuming you have read every word up until this point) and find where you are in your process of becoming an online entrepreneur. Take out pencil and paper, or start a new word processing document to make a plan for yourself. Start with a plan for your "big picture" goals and then chunk it down into what you need to do this week to begin. Perhaps you need to get hosting so that you can start a WordPress site. Or maybe you already have a site but need to start adding some content. Wherever you happen to be along the continuum is where you belong right now. Move forward one step and one day at a time. Slow and steady wins this race, as it is a marathon, not a sprint.

Over time you will get to the point where you have a daily, weekly, monthly, quarterly, and annual plan for your business. Anything further out than one year is overkill for online entrepreneurs, in my honest opinion. I never go to sleep at night without knowing what I will be doing the next day and for most of the upcoming week. I keep what I refer to as a "dynamic" to-do list, where everything I wish to accomplish is listed. My goal is to delegate what I cannot do, do not want to do, or am unable to do myself, to delete those tasks which are no longer a part of what I intend to do, and to accomplish everything else in a timely manner.

Find a mentor to guide you through the process of building a successful online business. I've included a link to my Online Marketing Incubator mentoring program in the resources section at the end of this book. Surrounding yourself with like-minded people and led by a strong mentor will make a huge difference for you.

Think about the two business models that make sense for you right now. I started with affiliate marketing and local business marketing before expanding to information product creation, membership sites, authorship and publishing, mentoring, live events, and selling physical products. Again, dip your toe in the water at first to find what appeals to you, and then move forward with a plan of action to propel you to success.

Once you get into the habit of doing what it takes every single day, you will raise the frequency of your vibration to a level that will astound you. What I mean by this is that you will move faster, think more deeply, and almost feel like you have superpowers. I could never go back to the way things were before and neither will you once you get moving in the proper direction for your goals.

Appendix

Productivity Challenge 2016

Since the spring of 2011 I have hosted an annual productivity challenge on my blog for my clients, mentees, and readers. I thought you would benefit from seeing what this is all about so I am including my 2016 Challenge in its entirety here.

This has been an excellent marketing strategy and you will gain some valuable insight into my business by studying what I have done here.

Attention: It's May of 2016 and please take this opportunity to jump in at any time for this Productivity Challenge. Take it at your own pace and ask me anything in the comments section. Connect with others also in the Challenge, and come back every day or two for updates.

It's that time of year again! Yes, I'm back for the sixth year with my Productivity Challenge, and this time I am anxious to bringing you the very best challenge you can imagine. Whether you are an aspiring online entrepreneur or a seasoned one you will find this year's productivity challenge 2016 to be both meaningful and a worthwhile use of your time and efforts. This time it will be a 30 day challenge so that you will get the most from it during the next month.

Day 1 - Your Digital Assets - Today I want you to make a list of your digital assets. By this I mean anything you have created out of electrons that is available on the internet for others to see, use, learn from, purchase, or recommend. For example, a list of my digital assets would include:

Books for Sale on Amazon - I have more than a dozen non-fiction books (paperback and Kindle) I have either written or contributed to, as well as one in a different genre that was completely outsourced. All of these books bring me regular income, build my list, and increase my credibility and visibility in the field of online marketing.

Information Products - I have more than fifty of these currently and increase them regularly. During this challenge we will discuss how to quickly create products to add to your online inventory.

Throughout this 20 Day Productivity Challenge receive a discount on my all new Really Simple Info Products training course. Leave a comment below and I'll contact you personally with details.

Online Training Courses - These are my favorite to create and teach. Because I was a classroom teacher for twenty years I'm always looking for ways to share my knowledge and expertise with others. This year I started my "Really Simple" branding and product/course line and committed to creating eight new online trainings during 2016.

Podcasts - I have two series, one where I interview others and one where I teach various aspects of online marketing. Both are available as subscriptions on iTunes. (More on this on Day 19)

YouTube Channel - Be ready for your close up by sharing short (less than five minutes is best) videos on your topic and your lifestyle.

Niche Sites - These are sites on various topics that recommend affiliate products.

My Mentor Programs - I offer an Online marketing Incubator, as well as a Platinum Mastermind Mentor Program.

Live Events - Twice a year I bring people together for a three day live event on some aspect of online marketing. Most recently these have been branded as "Weekend Marketer Live!"

Affiliate Recommendations - I have thousands of links to affiliate offers within the content I publish regularly.

Your Own Affiliate Program - I have about two hundred affiliates recommending my products, courses, and events regularly. Let me know if you are interested in becoming my affiliate, or take a look at AffiliateLinksandTools.com to get started today.

Short Reports, My Two Blogs, Teleseminars, Webinars, Press Releases, Social Media Profiles, Slide Presentations, and More -

This is content you have available online for your prospects to find, primarily by keyword but also through connections and relationships. This builds your credibility and visibility over time.

I'm not including physical products in this list, primarily because the Productivity Challenge 2016 is geared towards digital assets, with the exception of my books that are also available as paperback editions.

Commit to increasing your own digital assets exponentially over the next thirty days.

Are you surprised by how much or how little is on your list of digital assets?

Day 2 - Part 1 of What's for Sale? This is the magic question I ask my students regularly. You must fill your virtual shelves with digital inventory, and you own products, courses, programs, and events will always serve you most effectively. Think about what you currently have available for sale online, and what you would like to offer during the next month, six months, and within a year.

How will you get from where you are today to closer to where you would like to be? Who and what do you need to make this possible? Are you as productive each day as you would like to be? Why or why not?

Day 3 - Are You Working with a Mentor? I had a mentor during my first year online, and even though we were not the right fit for each other I saw the value in this concept. I went on to work with several mentors over the years, and currently I work with two - one is an online marketing expert and the other is a venture capitalist.

What is your position on this topic?

Day 4 - Writing and Publishing a Book made all of the difference for me in 2010. Soon I was being offered speaking engagements, more people wanted to join my Mentor programs, and my income took a huge leap. I was being taken more seriously and my credibility and visibility soared. Currently I am writing my fourteenth book, to be titled *Doing What It Takes*. It will be released during the summer of 2016. I spend one full hour each morning writing, and another fifteen minutes at night working on my outline in preparation for the following morning's writing. This enables me to write a full length book (about thirty-five thousand words) in four to six weeks, without giving up any of my other activities.

Are you a published author? If so, leave a comment below and tell us where we can find your book(s).

Day 5 - Massive Productivity - This 30 Day Productivity Challenge: 2016 is all about becoming more productive and focused on your journey as an online entrepreneur. Experience has taught me that the fastest path to success is by determining your *prime time* (the hours each day when you are most alert and ready to work) and then protecting those hours as many days a week as possible. My *prime time* hours are from about six in the morning until about ten or eleven in the morning, and I protect those hours at least four days each week. When I am writing a book or creating a new product or course, I protect that time six days a week until my project in well underway and moving forward in the direction I intended. Doing what I am describing here has allowed me to build an online empire that would not have been possible through any other method.

When is your prime time and are you protecting those hours as you build and grow your business?

Day 6 - Part 2 of What's For Sale? If I were ready to purchase everything you have for sale online right now - digital products, courses, programs, coaching, etc. - what would I find from you today? And remember that it only truly counts if it is on a separate domain with a sales page and buy buttons. I have about sixty items available, ranging in price from seven dollars to more than ten thousand. This didn't happen overnight, but instead in a steady, methodical way based on the marketing strategies I continue to use and improve upon.

I use PLR (private label rights) content for many of my products.

This is content created for the purpose of using as your own with full ownership rights. Here are the people and sites I recommend:

- Alice Seba - ConnieLoves.me/FreePLR
- Ronnie Nijmeh - ConnieLoves.me/SelfHelpPLR
- Coaching Sticky Glue - CoachingStickyGlue.com
- Alice Seba & Ron Douglas - ConnieLoves.me/9Templates
- Dennis Becker - ConnieLoves.me/8Reports

What questions may I answer for you about this?

Day 7 - What's Your Plan? Are you making plans for the remainder of this year in regards to your business? Goal setting and planning for the week, month, quarter, and year must be a part of your strategy as an online entrepreneur. Take some time right now to map out a plan for product creation, your own learning, reading, coaching, affiliate marketing, list building, live events, and anything else that is a part of your business.

Share any parts of this you would like to in the comments section.

Day 8 - Your Primary Focus(es) - You must have a primary focus to build a successful business, I honestly believe. For example, right now my primary focuses are to finish writing my next book - Doing What It Takes - and to continue my Really Simple series of products and courses, one at a time. Every day I spend time working on both of these before I do anything else. This translates to me working on these two projects before I check email, eat breakfast, exercise, speak with my students, send out an email to my list, or anything else. By eight in the morning I have usually accomplished more than I used to by noon or after before I insisted on being massively productive.

What is your primary focus right now and how often are you willing to spend time working on it?

Day 9 - Blogging - Blogging has been around since right before I came online more than ten years ago. A blog (short for web log) is a website where you are able to speak your mind in writing, get your message out to the world, find your voice, and market yourself and your business. A definition of blogging is: *a regularly updated website or web page, typically one run by an individual or small group, that is written in an informal or conversational style.* The fact that the search engines love blogs when they are rich with updated and relevant content means that you and I have a platform in which to have an online presence that we own and control.

I have maintained two blogs, this one and ConnieRagenGreen.com since coming online and benefit in many ways from both of them. They also host my two podcasts, which is yet another way to build your business as an online entrepreneur. My first book, *Huge Profits With a Tiny List: 50 Ways to Use Relationship Marketing to Increase Your Bottom Line*, started out as fifty blog posts I repurposed into chapters and sections of that book. When people search for us these days, they typically type our name into Google and look for our blog to learn more about us and what we have to offer. This is beneficial if you take the time to set it up and maintain your content.

Make sure you are using "hosted" WordPress as your platform, and not a free one. I recommend BlueHostSolutions.com for this so you can get started in the right direction.

Are you blogging regularly? Leave a comment below with a link to your site so that we may all take a look.

Day 10 - Content Creation - Are you creating content in written, audio, and video formats on a regular basis? It's so important to get your name and voice out to the world so that others think of you as three dimensional, whether they have met you in person or not. I recommend blogging and articles for your written content, teleseminars and podcasts for audio content, and videos and webinars for your video content. I do all of these regularly and am happy to answer your questions, address your challenges, and share my best resources with you so that you may move forward with your business quickly.

What are your questions regarding content creation, audio, or video? How are you using these to expand your business exponentially?

We are one third of the way through the Productivity Challenge 2016! Hooray!

Day 11 - Landing Pages - These are also called optin pages, "shy yes" pages, or squeeze pages. The goal is to target different segments of your target audience with free giveaways that make sense for them. Over the years I have set up about fifty of these, and the results have been nothing short of phenomenal.

Do you have these types of pages set up to build your list and expand your audience? What questions do you have for me about this marketing strategy?

Day 12 - Networking Online - Connecting with people online is very similar to how we do it online, with one exception; you are able to connect with people a thousand times faster over the internet than in person. Spend time each week in making a list of the people you would like to know better and then reach out to them via email and social media. I started doing this with the people I had purchased from, making sure to tell them what I liked most about their product and course and how I had benefited from it. Then I asked if I could interview them about how they got started as an entrepreneur. Over the past five years these have become podcasts, and I now count as my friends and colleagues some of the smartest people working online today.

Are you reaching out to those in your niche who have been online for many years? If not, why not? If so, what do you do after your initial connection to make sure the relationship blossoms?

Day 13 - Affiliate Marketing - This was my first business model when I began as an online entrepreneur. It allowed me to observe the entire process of how a product was launched and marketed, as well as how the product creator handled customer service. I thought of it as my "earn while you learn" program. It's funny now, but in the beginning I thought I would only promote affiliate products and services until I had products of my own. And then as I created my own I was quick to realize that affiliate marketing would always make sense. This income stream currently accounts for about forty percent of my income each year, and I continue to enjoy the process of recommending what I love to those who come to me as their trusted advisor.

Are you doing any affiliate marketing as you build your business? Have you read my popular, bestselling book on this topic or taken my Really Simple Affiliate Marketing training course?

Day 14 - Are You a Risk Taker? If you define yourself as an entrepreneur, the notion of taking risks is inherent in that label. The definition of an entrepreneur is *a person who organizes and operates a business or businesses, taking on greater than normal financial risks in order to do so.*

I can remember when I got started investing in real estate when I was in my early twenties. Someone who mentored me with this asked me if I was "risk averse". I determined right then and there that I would not be reluctant to get involved with a property even if it seemed like a long shot to earn a profit. This enabled me to get involved with deals that others shied away from and to walk away with some hefty profits.

When I came online I walked away from a twenty year career as a classroom teacher, and then I cash out my entire retirement account in order to have the money to live while I was building this business.

Along with the risk of entrepreneurship comes the great rewards, and taking responsibility for everything that occurs is a part of this.

What are your thoughts on risk taking as a part of being an online entrepreneur? What questions may I answer for you along these lines?

Day 15 - Perfectionism - Mark Cuban, owner of the Dallas Mavericks professional basketball team, Shark Tank panelist, and entrepreneur extraordinaire says that "perfection is the enemy of the entrepreneur". I am a recovering perfectionist myself, so I know what it's like to be paralyzed into inaction for fear of something being less than perfect while on our watch.

The way I overcame this so that I could stat and grow my business was to build up my confidence and not care what almost everyone else thought about what I was doing. This freed me up to be creative and to take risks I otherwise would not have taken. Now I see that I limited my success throughout my childhood and into my adult years by attempting to be perfect or not do things at all.

I have recently published a coloring book called Coloring for Perfectionists in an attempt to help others overcome this destructive trait. It's part of my new *Color My World Outside the Lines* series.

What questions do you have about perfectionism? Is this an area you have had to deal with in your life and/or your business? What do you suggest as a way to overcome it?

We are now halfway through Productivity Challenge 2016!

Day 16 - Choosing a Niche - As you build your online business you will want to have two niches; one for your Core business and another for experimentation. I started out by helping others write, publish and market their eBooks as my primary, core niche and small dog training as the niche based on something I knew and loved where I could experiment with what I was learning each day. The result was that I developed even more secondary niches and was able to supplement my core niche with the skills I had honed on the sites fewer people would see. I lost myself in these niches without feeling self conscious about what they looked like or if I made mistakes. Additionally, this increased my income over time as I learned how to choose lucrative niches far away from the online marketing space. It helped me to remember that internet marketing is a tiny niche compared to so many others.

For my Really Simple Info Products training course I choose yet another niche in which to create a new digital product. This will serve as an example to my students as to what can be achieved online, no matter what your level of experience with online marketing and information product creation. Any niche in which you have some experience or training, as well as a passion or keen interest can be monetized and added as a stream of residual income.

Do you have at least one other niche besides the one where you are building your primary, Core business? Have you monetized it? What questions do you have for me in the area of choosing your niche?

Day 17 - The way you do anything is the way you do everything. I was first introduced to this concept as a part of a personal development program I went through right before coming online in 2006. After some research I see that it can be traced back to musician Tom Waits in 1999. This turned me into a student of human behavior and someone who observes the interactions between people to find out what they are really about. I will use myself as an example here.

In my previous life as a classroom teacher and real estate broker/appraiser I was not willing to do what it takes to rise above the fray. By this I mean that I did what was required and expected of me, but typically no more than that. I could be counted on to finish assignments on time and turn in work that was acceptable, but I did not go above and beyond that level. It is no wonder that I did not achieve the results I was dreaming on in my life or my business; I wasn't willing to stretch that far. The way I did anything each and every day was the way I was doing everything. Ten years ago my eyes opened up to this and I began my concerted effort to change. These days I look for ways to do things in a more excellent (not perfect) manner and my results continue to pay off in a major way.

Observe your own thinking on this, as well as your behavior and the results you are manifesting.

What are your thoughts on the topic of "how we do anything is the way we do everything"?

Day 18 - Building Your Team - Behind every successful entrepreneur is a team of smart and talented people. Your goal is to find the right people for you and build relationships with them that are win-win.

I knew on my first day online I would need help with the

technical side of this business, as well as someone to create graphics and other visual objects. Fortunately I met someone almost right away who was excellent at both and we worked together for a couple of years. Over the years I have added mentors, accountability partners, virtual assistants, personal assistants, project managers, a bookkeeper, CPA, and others to my team.

Every single person who currently assists me is someone I met in person at a live event or charity function. Even though I work almost exclusively on the internet, the power of the face to face connection cannot be understated.

Who is on your team? Who are you looking for to round out your team? How may I assist you with this part of your online business?

Day 19 - Are You Podcasting? Even though I had been hosting teleseminars regularly since 2007, I did not jump on the podcasting bandwagon until 2011. Now that it's coming up on five years I'm not sure how I ever lived without utilizing this marketing strategy.

I actually have two separate podcasts, one that is an interview series and the other where I teach on topics I have become expert in over the years. Both of these are available on iTunes as free subscriptions, and are hosted on my two main WordPress sites, this one and at ConnieRagenGreen.com. Recently I released a product on how to set up your own podcast quickly and easily called Really Simple Podcasting.

No matter what your niche, podcasting makes sense. I have done these recordings from home and from locations all over the world as a way to stay connected with my community and to reach new listeners.

If you have a podcast, leave a comment below and tell us where we may find it. If you don't yet have a podcast, what questions may I answer for you on this topic?

Day 20 - Live Events - Do you plan to attend at least two live marketing events each year? During my first year and a half working online I honestly believed I could not possibly afford to do this. Once

I did, everything changed dramatically in my business. Looking back, it would have made sense to borrow the money, put it on a credit card, or even to sell something in order to finance these trips.

The cost of events has dropped considerably over the years. I continue to host my *Weekend Marketer Live* event twice a year and it is less than five hundred dollars to attend. I also pair people up as roommates for additional savings.

At live events you will connect with like-minded individuals, learn an incredible amount of useful information, and have the opportunity to spend time with people doing exactly what it is you would like to do as an online entrepreneur. I continue to attend other people's events, and over the past eight years have spoken at or attended more than eighty events, including more than a dozen of my own.

I also host Retreats in Santa Barbara several times each year. Groups of four or five people meet with me over a five day period to work on their businesses in a stress free, gorgeous beach community setting.

Which events have you attended? What type of events are you most attracted to? What questions may I answer for you around this topic?

Day 21 - List Building, Part 1 - I think of list building as a two part process; the first part involves attracting the right people to your site(s) and persuading them to exchange their email address for your irresistible free giveaway, while the second part is comprised of the relationship you will continue to build upon with them for the time they remain on your list. Both parts are equally valuable, yet each requires a very different series of actions.

Let's look at the first part, where someone (let's call them a visitor) arrives at your blog or optin page (also referred to as a squeeze page - see Page 11 above) and makes the hasty decision whether or not to join your list. Now they may have been referred to you and/or your site by a third party, but let's assume they found you by Googling a keyword phrase that led them to you. We have all been in this position on the internet. We are searching for information on a topic of interest to use and we end up on someone's site. How do we make that split second decision whether or not to opt in to the person's list or to click away and continue our search? I believe it's a

- The look and feel of the site either attracts or repels us. This happens on a subconscious level and is the most powerful force you will experience. It's that little voice in your head that either whispers "You've found exactly what you need to move forward" or shouts "Danger, danger, there's nothing here for you. Move on quickly and don't look back!" Yes, it is really this dramatic and worthy of further study to ensure you achieve more of the former than the latter in your online business.

- The free report or other information you are giving away to those who decide to opt in is a crucial part of this process. It must hit the mark in terms of providing your visitor the information they need to turn them into a prospect. This is no time to cut corners or to hold back on the knowledge you possess around your topic. Give them your best information, keep it concise, and know that by so doing you are setting yourself apart from almost everyone else working online today. If your free giveaway is truly irresistible, your list will grow quickly and steadily.

What questions do you have on the topic of attracting the right people to your site and creating a free giveaway that is irresistible?

Day 22 - List Building, Part 2 - Relationship Marketing -The second part of the list building process involves the ongoing process of relationship marketing. I became extremely effective with this early on in my career as an online entrepreneur and continue to teach and share my strategies with others. It all begins when someone chooses to opt in to your list. What happens immediately afterward will make or break your reputation and your business.

When we opt in to a list we are first taken to a thank you page or a confirmation page, depending upon how we have set it all up. Then our prospect (remember they have gone from visitor to prospect simply by giving us their name and email address) will check their email to download the free giveaway they were promised. *Delivering on this promise is a huge obligation and you must be willing to do whatever it takes to make it a positive and smooth experience for them.* I cannot emphasize this enough; not delivering on this promise in the most professional way is tantamount to missing a child's birthday or not returning a call to a dear, long-time friend. It's unforgivable and will not be tolerated at the beginning of a relationship.

Once you have made it through this initial stage of the relationship you now take on the role of trusted advisor on your area of expertise. Stay in regular contact through autoresponder and broadcast email messages, include relevant information, thought provoking ideas, and excellent resources (both paid and free) that will enhance your new prospect's experience and results. Your goal now is to turn them into a client as soon as possible.

What questions do you have for me during this part of the list building process? What are your experiences in this area?

Day 23 - Become a "Local Celebrity" - It was quite my accident during my first several years working exclusively online that people in my city began to recognize me and know what I was doing in my business. It started when I shared my new business ventures with the people in my Rotary Club and expanded when I discussed it with the other charities and non-profits I was a part of in my community. Soon I was being asked to speak to various groups and it didn't take long for me to be asked to write a column in a local publication and be a frequent guest on the radio show.

You can do the same exact thing, but do it on purpose instead of by accident. Let people know what you do and how you can best serve them with your knowledge and expertise. Accept all speaking engagements, knowing that they would not have asked you if they didn't feel strongly that you had something valuable to share. And also, send a press release to announce your accomplishments, such as releasing a new product or course, publishing a book, or being nominated for an award. All of what I am sharing with you here will help to catapult you to greater opportunities more quickly than you ever could have imagined.

Are you a local celebrity? Please share your thoughts and experiences on this topic with us in the comments below.

Day 24 - Public Speaking - I spoke previously about the importance of accepting any and all speaking engagements you are invited to. You may be wondering what you can do if you are not ever asked by others to speak to their groups. The answer is a simple one - host your own events and speak!

I have spoken all over the world, and many times I either invited myself or hosted my own events. When Joe Vitale was putting on an event in Austin, Texas in 2013, I called him to ask if I could be one of the featured speakers. He immediately said yes, and then quickly apologized for not thinking of this himself.

Remember that hosting your own webinars and teleseminars is also public speaking, and that local groups and organizations like Rotary are always looking for new and interesting speakers and topics. Introduce yourself and then ask for the microphone!

Are you already doing some public speaking? What are your thoughts on this marketing strategy?

Day 25 - Emailing Your List - Once you have even one person on your list, begin to get into the habit of sending email messages *at least* three times each week. This will feel awkward and intrusive at first, but you will soon feel comfortable with staying in touch at this level.

Emails sent out in real time are referred to as broadcasts and may be time sensitive in nature. Emails set up in advance to go out on a predetermined schedule are referred to as autoresponders. You will be using both of these in your business.

Remember that we train people how to behave with us, so make sure to include at least one clickable link in each email you send. And even though you may be tempted to only share tips, resources, and free items with your prospects they need to know from the first day that you are in business to earn an income.

I prefer text emails over HTML because not everyone has HTML enabled on all of their devices. With text emails you can be assured that everyone receiving them will be able to read every word you have written. I continue to use Aweber to send out the majority of my emails.

Do you have a list? Are you emailing them regularly to build your relationship with each person on your list? What questions do you have for me on this topic?

Day 26 - Short Reports - I started learning about writing, publishing, and marketing short reports from Jimmy D Brown when I was first on the internet and implemented what he taught very quickly. The idea was to include as much information as possible within a thirty or forty page report, and then to either sell or give away the short report to those who were interested in the topic.

Soon I began purchasing PLR (private label rights) content that I could repurpose into short reports within a few minutes. These were well written and contained much more information than I would be able to create myself that easily. I also started giving away these reports as a way to promote my own products and courses as well as those of affiliates. You can see the selection of short reports I currently have available for download at no cost over at ConnieRagenGreen.com in the tool bar near the top of the page.

I recommend that you write your own reports in the beginning to get the feel for this model, and then look above at **Page 6** of this *Productivity Challenge 2016* to connect with the people I go to for PLR.

What is your experience with Short Reports? What questions do you have for me on this lucrative business model?

Day 27 - Membership Sites - When I was first online there were only two choices when it came to setting up a membership site. Both platforms had price tags in the thousands of dollars, and you had to be very technically inclined or have access to a webmaster in order to maintain your sites. This was out of the question for me at that time, both due to it being cost prohibitive and the fact that my technology skills were limited at best.

Fast forward three years, to 2009 and I was in a Mastermind with a couple of very sharp individuals. They were Tracy Childers and Stu McLaren and they had an idea for a WordPress plugin that could turn your site into a membership site with a few mouse clicks. It was actually a little more involved than I am describing here, but it was easy enough for almost anyone to set up and maintain. They called it Wishlist Member and I was in on the ground floor as they launched this to the world.

I continue to use Wishlist on more than thirty of my sites. And there are more than a dozen models for using membership site software besides the ones that may come to mind. These include providing you with a secure, protected area to house and deliver content for a product or course, as well as a way to drip out content on your topic to members over a specific period of time or on an ongoing basis.

Membership sites can provide you with a recurring income stream that will grow larger over time.

Do you have a membership site for your business? What questions do you have about this part of the business model?

Day 28 - What's Your Story? - You can see by now that sharing more about who we are and what we stand for will be beneficial as we build our businesses. This is referred to as the art of storytelling and can be the reason you create a group of raving fans from the very beginning or fall into the habit of blending in with everyone else doing business online. Choose to stand out by sharing your story, and do not be modest.

I continue to share my lifestyle with my community, and this includes how I am able to live in two beautiful cities in southern California - Santa Clarita and Santa Barbara - simultaneously, my ongoing world travels, my extended family in Finland, and my experiences with Rotary and other non-profits.

Also, I share both my successes and failures, how I struggled with technology and writing when I first came online, and how I had to build up my confidence in order to believe in myself along the way. All of this adds up to my willingness to show vulnerability, imperfection, and just being human. And it gives my community the faith that they can do the same thing in their own way.

What's your story? Share it with us in the comments below.
Day 29 - Let's Get Social - The advent of social media changed everything for people wishing to do business online, but few seem to understand how to do this effectively. If I visit your social media pages, will I even know you are in business?

You must let your followers, friends, and connections on social media know who you are, what you do, and how you serve others. This is done strategically over time by sharing a part of yourself in relation to your business.

I would encourage you to visit your pages and profiles today to make sure your photo is current, your website is prominent, and you are keeping your comments and postings professional and interesting. This will pay off handsomely over time.

Where can we find you on social media?

Day 30 - Your Own Challenge! - On this final day of the Productivity Challenge 2016 I invite you to start a challenge of your own. What I didn't tell you back on Day 9 when we talked about blogging was that I started the very first Blogging Challenge in 2008. It started out very slowly, with people leaving comments on my blog post about it and including a link to their most recent post. Over time it picked up steam, and now hundreds of people (these are only the ones I know about) host their own blogging challenges regularly.

No matter what type of challenge is of interest to you, jump in and begin! I recommend a seven or fourteen day challenge as your first one. This will allow you to get a feel for challenges so that you can see what is most effective for your niche topic. Be sure to purchase a domain name, as I have done here, to forward to the permalink of your challenge post. And let me know where it is so I may stop by and support your efforts.

What questions do you have on this topic and how may I best support you now and in the future?

NOTE: Did you notice how I have a separate domain

(ProductivityChallenge2016.com) for this post? It's a simple way for me to create a five to six thousand word free product to use as a Special Report in the future. This strategy is both effective and profitable!

You may want to visit my site (this exact post can be found at ProductivityChallenge2016.com) to spend more time with this, and to leave a comment. If you are just starting out as an online entrepreneur, host a seven or fourteen day challenge and promote it through social media. It does not matter if you do not receive any comments this first time. The important aspect of this strategy is in moving forward in a way that can catapult you to great success over time.

Resources

A single conversation with a wise man during the eating of a meal, is better than ten years' mere study of books.
~ Chinese Proverb

Here are some of my most valuable resources to help you get your online business up and running quickly:

My Mentor Program - http://TheOnlineMarketingIncubator.com

My Most Recent Teleseminar http://AskConnieAnything.com

My Main Sites
http://ConnieRagenGreen.com
http://HugeProfitsTinyList.com

My Two Podcasts
Interview Series:
        http://itunes.apple.com/us/podcast//id494678649
Online Marketing Tips:
        http://itunes.apple.com/us/podcast//id591740909

Productivity Challenge 2016
http://ProductivityChallenge2016.com

Website and Blog Hosting
http://BlueHostSolutions.com

Autoresponder and Broadcast Emails
http://ConnieLoves.me/Aweber

Become my Affiliate
http://AffiliateLinksandTools.com

Press Releases
http://WebWire.com

Autoresponder E-Course
http://AutoresponderECourse.com

Membership Site Plugin
http://ConnieLoves.me/Wishlist

Many of the resources I am recommending to you here are through my affiliate link, meaning that I will receive compensation should you decide to purchase them. Know that I do not take this relationship lightly, and that I stand behind everything I recommend to you and to others personally.

Reading List

If you only read the books everyone else is reading, you can only think what everyone else is thinking.
~ Haruki Murakami

I believe that we must give ourselves a business education by reading books from a variety of authors. I've included some recent favorites here and encourage you to read on an ongoing basis for the rest of your life. And I'd love it if you would share your favorites with me so that I may be exposed to new ideas and ways of thinking about life and business.

Grit to Great: How Perseverance, Passion, and Pluck Take You from Ordinary to Extraordinary by Linda Kaplan Thaler and Robin Koval

#AskGaryVee: One Entrepreneur's Take on Leadership, Social Media, and Self-Awareness by Gary Vaynerchuk

The School of Greatness: A Real-World Guide to Living Bigger, Loving Deeper, and Leaving a Legacy by Lewis Howes

Miracle Morning: The Not-So-Obvious Secret Guaranteed to Transform Your Life (Before 8AM) by Hal Elrod

Living Forward: A Proven Plan to Stop Drifting and Get the Life You Want by Michael Hyatt

The 12 Week Year: Get More Done in 12 Weeks Than Others Do in 12 Months by Brian P. Moran and Michael Lennington

The Difference: How Anyone Can Prosper in Even the Toughest Times by Jean Chatzky

The Power of Habit: Why We Do What We Do in Life and Business by Charles Duhigg

The One Thing: The Surprisingly Simple Truth Behind Extraordinary Results by Gary Keller

The Slight Edge: Turning Simple Disciplines Into Massive Success and Happiness by Jeff Olson and John David Mann

Fierce Conversations: Achieving Success at Work and in Life One Conversation at a Time by Susan Scott

The Compound Effect: Jumpstart Your Income, Your Life, Your Success by Darren Hardy

The Millionaire Next Door: The Surprising Secrets of America's Wealthy by Thomas J. Stanley and William D. Danko

Feel the Fear and Do It Anyway by Susan Jeffers

What To Say When You Talk To Yourself by Shad Helmstetter

And all of my books are available at: ConnieRagenGreenBooks.com

About the Author

Connie Ragen Green is a bestselling author, publisher, international speaker, and online marketing strategist. She divides her time between two California cities - Santa Clarita in the desert and Santa Barbara at the beach.

In addition to writing, speaking, and publishing, Connie also enjoys spending time traveling the world and staying involved with a variety of non-profit organizations. This began when she joined Rotary, an international service organization, in 2006 and has now expanded to work with Zonta, Elk's, Boy's & Girl's Club, and The American Cancer Society, to name a few.

Connie's dream is to visit a remote village in one of the few remaining countries where polio is still endemic and to help administer the vaccine to those most at risk.

Made in the USA
San Bernardino, CA
15 February 2018